MESSAGES FROM SPIRIT

MESSAGES FROM SPIRIT

Breathtaking insights into life and the afterlife

GEORGINA WALKER

ALLEN&UNWIN
SYDNEY • MELBOURNE • AUCKLAND • LONDON

First published in 2013

Copyright © Georgina Walker 2013

All rights reserved. No part of this book may be reproduced or transmitted in any form or by any means, electronic or mechanical, including photocopying, recording or by any information storage and retrieval system, without prior permission in writing from the publisher. The Australian *Copyright Act 1968* (the Act) allows a maximum of one chapter or 10 per cent of this book, whichever is the greater, to be photocopied by any educational institution for its educational purposes provided that the educational institution (or body that administers it) has given a remuneration notice to Copyright Agency Limited (CAL) under the Act.

Inspired Living, an imprint of Allen & Unwin
83 Alexander Street
Crows Nest NSW 2065
Australia
Phone: (61 2) 8425 0100)
Email: info@allenandunwin.com
Web: www.allenandunwin.com

Cataloguing-in-Publication details are available
from the National Library of Australia
www.trove.nla.gov.au

ISBN 978 1 74237 016 3

Set in 12.25/18 pt New Caledonia by Bookhouse, Sydney
Printed and bound in Australia by Griffin Press

10 9 8 7 6 5 4 3 2 1

MIX
Paper from responsible sources
FSC® C009448

The paper in this book is FSC® certified. FSC® promotes environmentally responsible, socially beneficial and economically viable management of the world's forests.

To my very precious grandchildren, Jade, Mikaela, Claira and Jack—tomorrow's intuitives!

All but a handful of names have been changed.

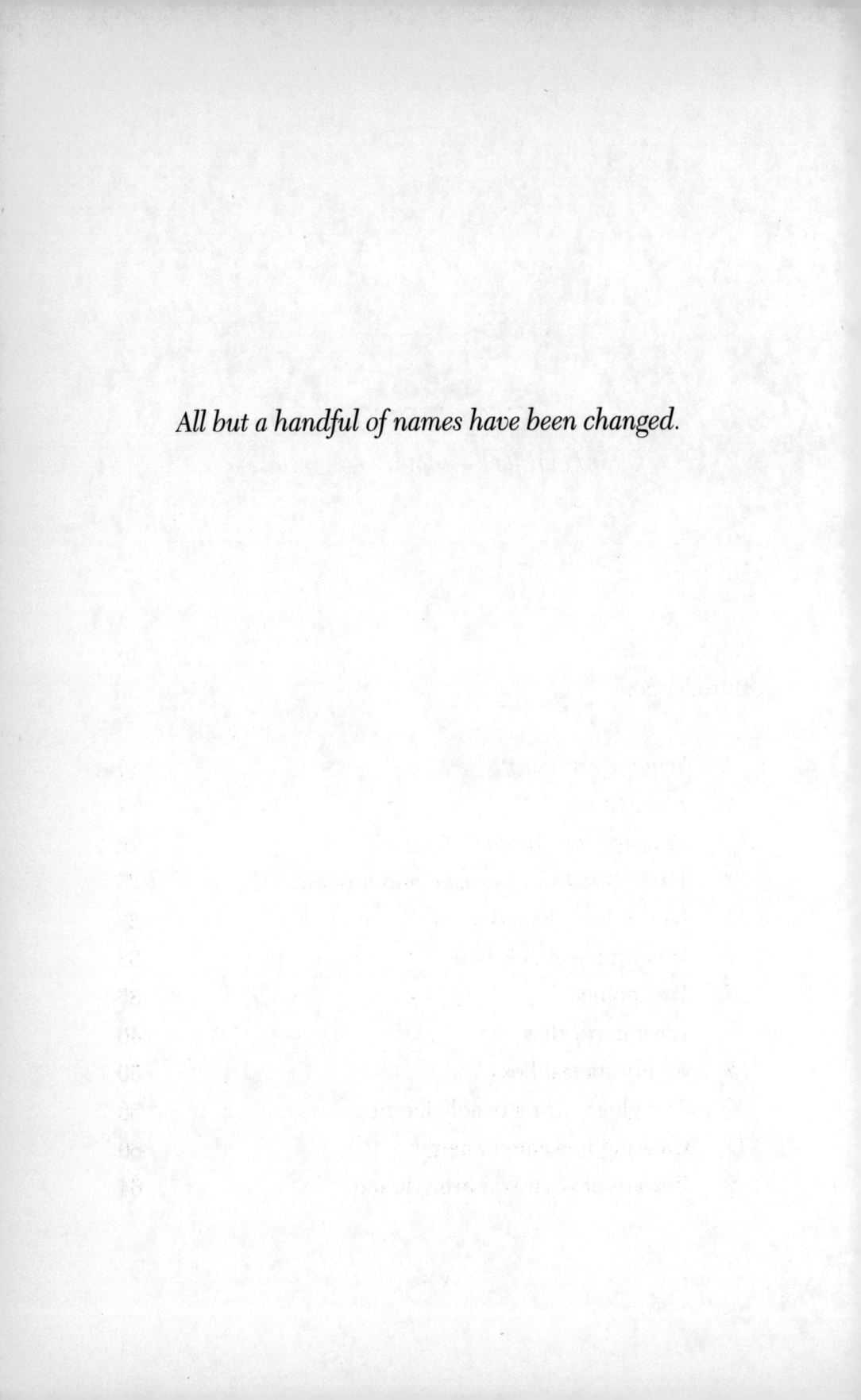

CONTENTS

Appreciation ix
Introduction xi

1 When spirit talks 1
2 Scary times 7
3 Reaching out beyond the grave 16
4 Protection from the seen and unseen 23
5 Out of body experiences 28
6 When time stands still 33
7 Exit points 36
8 Love never dies 40
9 A very special box 50
10 The ghost with a deadly intent 56
11 Clearing unwanted energy 60
12 Beware of what you bring home 64

13	Seriously bad vibes	75
14	A message in the mirror	81
15	Gone but not forgotten	84
16	Unwelcome touch	94
17	Daring to do the impossible	99
18	Set in stone	107
19	Real life magic	113
20	Spirits in kind	120
21	My spirit companion	126
22	Ancient city, ancient secrets	130
23	Fallen soldiers	136
24	When spirit comes calling	141
25	Full circle	152
26	The pilgrimage	162
27	The secret of Bethlehem	168

Resources 175

APPRECIATION

We are surrounded by team builders—these are the earthly folk and our spiritual support team, who are there to energise, encourage and be enthusiastic when needed. I am in awe of you all! Thank you for being there.

Maggie Hamilton from Inspired Living at Allen & Unwin, who lovingly massages her authors with strokes of kindness, support and nurturing—once again you have been there for this, my third book. Many, many thanks for your belief in the workings of spirit-inspired literature.

All my wonderful friends and associates, locally and internationally, who presented amazing opportunities, adventures and resources for these stories.

Sabina Collins for your magic touch in editing my manuscript—big hugs and thanks.

INTRODUCTION

Hidden in some mysterious place within your being lies your soul, attuning and aligning its essence to the vibration of your heart. For within each beat comes a stirring of memories of the past, an understanding of the present and a knowingness of what is to come.

Everything living houses a soul—a lifelong companion that will detach and depart from the body at the point of physical death. For the soul does not die, it has a mission, a destiny to take the obligatory pilgrimage of soul to spirit, spirit to soul.

But do all souls take the same transformational path from this world to the next?

What is the next world?

Will a soul have free will over their journey?

Is there a choice between heaven, hell and an alternative—limbo?

If there exists no free will, is the decision made by a superior being—a cosmic mind who passes final judgement based on good over evil?

Are our cries for help and divine intervention heard by the soul? Or is the soul required to have returned to its source as spirit/guide before it can intercede?

What of the people who bargained with or sold their souls with the hope of obtaining material pleasures, at the cost of foregoing heaven, nirvana and utopia? What is their ultimate price?

Can a soul have such a powerful emotional connection to a person, personality or place that it is able to imprint itself onto its surroundings or individuals in a way that can be sensed and seen by others as hauntings, ghosts, toxic energy dumps, residual energy fields or possession?

The following true stories will take you on your own investigation; you will come up with your own theories, solutions and summations. But more importantly, as you read and know that the truth is out there, consider what legacy your soul will contribute and leave on this earth plane. Will it be retribution over those who have wronged you? Good deeds over evil ones? Make your choice wisely, as history has a way of repeating itself!

1

WHEN SPIRIT TALKS

There's no two ways about it, I have an interesting life. I love helping people through their grief by connecting them with loved ones on the other side. I guess you could say I talk to dead people. I talk to those who have died of natural causes or in accidents, to those who have suicided, or to those whose life was over before it had really begun. It's a gift I was born with. It's also a gift I kept to myself for a long time, because people were reluctant to talk about anything out of the ordinary.

But even in the years when I didn't own up to being a psychic intuitive, I was in regular contact with spirit. I got to see firsthand just how amazing this limitless world really is. Once I learned how, I did talk to those who had passed over. I also learned that our connection with spirit is much bigger than this. I came to see how much guidance there is for us out there, if and when we're prepared to listen.

Like all talents, my psychic abilities were something I needed to work on. I had to learn to reach out to spirit and to hear what it had to say to me. I also had to learn to trust the guidance I got. So you could say that my life as a psychic evolved. Spirit pushed me into trusting the messages I was given and to see how important this was if I hoped to use my intuitive skills.

I had been aware of my psychic gift from the age of seven. I was lucky because my parents understood and nurtured my gift. Most kids in my situation aren't so lucky and end up feeling very alone and misunderstood. Spirit has many ways of talking to us. The biggest challenge for spirit is to find ways to get our attention. I frequently had meaningful dreams, visions and mystical experiences, which gave me insights into my life and the lives of those around me. These messages were openly discussed in my childhood home, but what did they mean?

For my fifth birthday I was given a huge doll with dark hair and magic brown eyes. She was nearly as big as me and difficult to carry around. My parents were keen for me to give her a name, so I named her there and then: Betty. It seemed to satisfy their need that she have an identity. Later that day I was sitting on the verandah combing Betty's hair when I heard a spirit man's voice. It was an audible voice; you know, like the voice you hear from a distance when your parents are calling you to come home for dinner. I knew, I just knew, the voice was for me. I had a feeling inside that it felt right and knew not to be afraid.

He told me I should call my doll Carlotta, as that name had been important to me when I lived a life before. When I told my parents

I had changed the doll's name, I distinctly remember Mum asking me where on earth I had come up with a strange one like that! I will always remember the expression on Mum and Dad's faces when I explained how the spirit man had given me the message. Mum then said that it was right to call my doll Carlotta and if I ever had any more experiences with the spirit man or heard voices, I should tell her and she would write them down. And that was that, no further discussion was needed.

Shortly after this mystical encounter I heard words that were not in English. When I told my dad, he said the words were Hebrew but gave no further explanation. Growing up in that environment, my experiences with spirit were all so matter-of-fact. I now see how fortunate I was when I look back at my early apprenticeship to spirit—my parents were wise and open to the development of my gifts but I was not treated more specially because I had them. My childhood remained normal and loving, with no pressure to develop unnaturally quickly or to perform. It was a home of love, where psychic development was shaped and developed, no different than learning to use a knife and fork. It became automatic, escalating rapidly to me having visions at the age of seven, following a bout of rheumatic fever.

As I came to trust my gift, which had been honed over the years, I began doing psychic readings as a hobby from home. I'd swap a reading for a facial, a haircut or even for a pair of school shoes for one of my kids. It made life easier and I loved what I did. The gift developed rapidly when I moved to the outback, where life was far from easy. My mum used to say we're often more switched on to our natural-born abilities when we're stressed and that it gives us a helping hand when we need it most.

As the saying goes, use it or lose it. Over time I came to see that spirit talks to us in all kinds of ways, and has different messages for each of us. Some messages will be about everyday stuff. Some will help us with relationships or with health matters. Others will help us with work or even with ground-breaking research. Molecular biologist James Watson dreamed of a spiral staircase, leading him to the discovery of the double-helix component of the structure of DNA. Cultures that have an affinity with nature know the significance of dreams, omens and signs; it's key to their survival.

Sleep time is spirit time—a time when your angels and spirit guides can shape your dreams to give you solutions, answers to your needs. There is much truth in the adage about not going to bed on an argument, as your energies are not positive. I believe that the old-fashioned practice of saying a prayer prior to falling asleep has much wisdom in preparing the subconscious mind for visitations from the spirit world. I will give you some great tips as the book progresses on how to prepare and open yourself to the world of spirit in your dream state.

The gifts of spirit are at our disposal if we continue to use these amazing faculties that we were born with. The full-on lives we're now leading don't always help us join the dots. I worry that we will eventually lose our intuition, which is basically our survival gene. In my work I often find it's only through tragedy that many people start to wake up and believe. One of the secrets to keeping our intuition alive is to never stop learning. Using both the right and left hemispheres of our brain, and being curious about how this amazing world of ours works, we can use this natural computer to its fullest power and potential.

Alison is a great example of this. She has a Masters in Psychotherapy and is an energy worker with a dynamic and very busy practice. But in spite of her impressive qualifications, she felt a compelling need to evolve more as an individual, with the anticipation that the skills learned could be incorporated into the healing arts of her practice. Over the years Alison has made trips into the jungles of Colombia to study with the very wise shamans to learn more of their healing art. She has successfully merged her newly heightened intuition with that of her logical formal training to aid in the healing of her clients, many of whom present with feelings of emptiness that she believes stems from a lack of spiritual belief or foundation.

This is the perfect time for us to connect to spirit, because in spite of all our money and technology and everything else we have, we're not happy. I see this every day. I'm witnessing a trend among the many people I work with, from academics through to housewives and young adults, who are seriously disenchanted with life and society. It's not that they're wanting to opt out, but they want a life that amounts to more than sex and shopping and worrying about their wrinkles. They're looking for ways to enhance their lives so that they feel good about getting up in the morning.

On a deeper level, without them perhaps realising it at first, they're wanting to get in touch with their natural-born abilities of perception, intuition, foresight and dreams, to enrich their creativity and passion, and in some cases their inventive abilities. These are the people who hunger for something more—something that will not only enrich their lives and those of their families but contribute to and sustain a more productive world. These are tomorrow's people also who are ready to step into the future because they know the universe will help them do what they're meant to do and be where they're meant to be.

I have no doubt this universal urge to work with nature is aligned to the big changes the planets and our world are going through right now. And those who are choosing to tap into their natural-born abilities and gifts will be able to flow with these changes, which will stand us in good stead. Isn't this where you'd rather be? Sometimes we worry what others might think, but that's also part of the process. I'm going to help you join the dots, to help you make life more magical and more fulfilled.

2

SCARY TIMES

My gift has taken me on some amazing adventures, some of which I will share in the following chapters, but life hasn't always been so easy. In the early 1980s, life was hard, damn hard. I was married to a farmer and we struggled with isolation, drought, mice plagues and extreme financial hardship, all while raising four children from previous marriages and our own fifth child. My husband had only known farming. He was married to the land. His family and forefathers were all the same. Tradition dictated how they would work the earth and change was considered only in desperate times. One followed order, the seasons, and there was never time to consider something that you couldn't see or touch.

I recall one particular morning, while my hard-nosed rural husband was scoffing his breakfast, I declared: 'We must buy cattle—that's what my dream told me.' This was a big call. We were in drought. The paddocks were bare. We were hand-feeding the sheep with hay. We had started to cart water to partly fill the dams for stock and our own personal use. But now they resembled mud pools. The slush pumped from the dam to our holding tank, then into our bath, made the children cry. It smelled of dead sheep. The same water was used by two adults and four children. I would go to the local town park and fill up multiple plastic bottles, eskies and whatever else I could use to carry home fresh clean water for cooking and drinking.

Spirit does guide us, but it also requires us to have courage and faith. On the surface of it, what I was proposing was insane. How on earth would we be able to sustain cattle? There was, however, some money I had put aside, so very reluctantly my husband took me to the saleyards. He was embarrassed that I bid for six of the poorest looking Hereford crosses he had ever seen, and I spent $75 a head. They were so thin they all fitted into the back of a double horse float. But within the next three months we had great rain and subsequent feed, and I sold the cattle for $165 each. The profit was exactly the amount needed for our next repayment on the farm loan; no more, no less. It was a miracle—we were surviving when other farms were not, all thanks to a dream!

Spirit is the grand master of design, like a tailor fashioning an outfit with just the right amount of expensive fabric. Spirit will move the pattern pieces around to produce the finest garment without wastage. The same is true about how exact spirit is with energy—there is no waste. When we listen and act, the universe reveals more.

'Buy sheep!' were the words I heard upon waking one morning. By this time my marriage was not in good shape and as I talked about buying sheep, the older four children looked up in fear, expecting their father to explode. True, I knew nothing about buying sheep, but I had helped in the yards with vaccinations and shearing. I just needed a bit of advice about what kind of sheep I should buy for our land. So I boldly asked my husband, 'If you won't come with me, would you at least tell me what would you buy?'

'Aged Merino ewes joined to Border Leicesters,' was the harsh reply.

After the children went to school, I packed my baby son in the car and set off to the sales. I was silently praying all the way that a guardian angel would appear to guide me on my purchase. In hindsight, I didn't look the part: dressed in a lemon skirt, lemon and white checked shirt, porcelain flower earrings and high heels, with a baby in tow!

I saw a red-haired man in the pen inspecting the teeth of some ewes to determine their age and I asked him if they were pregnant. He stopped what he was doing, came over to the railing and asked what on earth I was doing there. I vividly remember my response: 'Today I am stepping out in faith—I want to prove a city woman can do anything a country man can.' He liked my attitude and told me that the ewes were definitely in lamb (pregnant) but not to pay more than $11 per head.

When the time came for the auction, I was on my own with the baby, surrounded by a whole lot of farmers. Just like an angel, the man who gave me the advice appeared beside me and said he would care for my son during the auction. Then he reminded me not to go above $11. The bidding began and I eventually purchased my pen of ewes for $8 each. 'You did real good,' a voice behind me said, as the farmer returned my son. 'Well done.' And with that, he disappeared into the crowd.

Then the stock agent wanted me to nominate who was taking the sheep home. I thought I only needed a small truck as I only had a small load. The agent laughed. 'You've bought nearly 400 sheep,' he said and abruptly walked away. I started to cry. I had the money to pay for them, but I didn't know the first thing about transporting a huge number of stock back to the farm.

Out of nowhere once again appeared my red-haired guardian angel. 'Now what's the matter?' he said. I explained the situation, after which he asked for the property's address and whether I wanted them penned in the holding yard there. My friend then told me to go and do my shopping and said that by the time I got home they would be there. He was true to his word. When I arrived home there were the sheep, all penned in the holding yards.

Months passed and my 400 ewes—all of them—dropped twins and triplets, and I made a massive profit! Once again the money I had spent was returned many times over and all the bills were up to date.

Several months had elapsed with no invoice for transport of the sheep arriving, so I rang the freight company and explained the reason for my call. The woman on the phone was amazed, as farmers never ask to pay their bills. There was silence for some time while she checked her records before she informed me that there was no money owing on the account. I still often wonder if the red-haired guardian angel had brought the sheep to the farm himself or if he had paid my bill.

It wasn't the straw that broke the camel's back; rather, the final straw was the goats! I had a dream to buy goats. This project actually appealed to my husband, though he wasn't paying for them. Goats were fashionable at the time and he liked to stand out from his farming neighbours by trying something different. I did my research. The Department of Agriculture advised that angora goats were unsuitable for our land; there were too many burrs, which would affect the quality of the fleece. But that's not what my guidance was telling me. I've now learned that the wisdom from the world of spirit is counter-intuitive—sometimes it asks you to do the opposite of what's considered the usual or rational way to go. What was I to do? Angora goats were expensive—very expensive—but I had enough money saved up to buy young weaners fresh off their mothers' milk, 30 in fact, plus some older, half-cross angoras.

I fell in love with the goats' personalities and their love of human contact, and so did my whole family. As the goats grew, their frames were larger than the average for their breed. I was told that it was due to the condition of the land and feed. Before long, some of the neighbouring farms had followed in our footsteps and gone into the goat business. Fashion was dictating the need for more angora fleece and the prices were indeed very high for the first soft cuts of their hair. I even went away and did a mohair classing course.

When it was time to shear their fleece, my husband was in one hell of a mood. He said the only way he would shear the goats was if we worked right through. That meant I couldn't stop to feed the baby. He was a hard man. I put our son in his stroller and silently prayed that he would sleep through the shearing.

The searing heat was magnified as we worked under the iron roof. It was going to be a long, hot day. There was no choice—we needed to get the hair to market. Then suddenly there was a cry of pain.

'I have to stop, my back's gone,' my husband yelled. He'd wrenched his back.

'You can't stop, we made a deal. You have to finish the run,' I pleaded, but to no avail. Silently, though, I was thanking the spirits above as I was relieved to end the torturous work.

One night soon after I had another dream: sell the goats now. Speaking up about the best way forward for the goats was not well received. My husband loved being the centre of progressive farming in the community. But the goats belonged to me, and it was my choice—our goat-farming days were over. Several agents looked at the animals and a deal was struck. I must admit I did cry when the goats left. However, I was pleased when the new owners actually rang and asked if we had any more goats to sell as they were so impressed with the quality! Within two weeks the bottom fell out of the mohair market and our stock would have been worthless. The sale had come just at the right time.

Life on the farm was hard. What I learned from my experience with the cattle and sheep was that I needed to take action. It was scary going into unfamiliar territory. But I knew the universe expects us to meet it halfway, so I needed to be courageous and step out of my comfort zone.

The struggle to feed and educate my children still continued after I left the marriage and rural life behind and moved to the city. But at least we had running water, I was making friends and the children were excited to have access to many options not available in a remote community. At times I was working five jobs, but I was content with my life, which was improving a little bit each day.

One day I had a dream that changed my life—I woke suddenly to hear a voice telling me: 'You can't love anyone else until you love yourself. Give yourself a present.' Boy, did I want to know what that present was! I fell back to sleep and was visited by a beautiful Asian woman, who later would become a powerful spirit guide in my life as a psychic intuitive. She showed me I would visit the 'Land of the Swords', where there was much work for me to do. She told me I wasn't to worry about money—it would come. I had learned so much on the farm about trusting my dreams, my guides and the lessons I had been taught. Memories stirred once again, reminding me about just how far I had come from those hardship days.

We all have times that stretch us to the limit. I know that my life would have been a lot harder without this guidance from spirit. It's often our toughest times that teach us most.

Looking back, a lot of my guidance over those years came in my sleep. This happens to a lot of people, but sadly many don't take any notice of the guidance they receive. The wonderful world of spirit moves when our mind chatter ceases. It's a great window that opens in our dreams. Perhaps an answer, a solution or a premonition may come, so always keep pen and paper by your bed. If you are woken during the night from a dream, no matter now minimal the information or vision may be, immediately write down what you saw and experienced, including the emotions you felt. In time the pieces of the puzzle that you receive in your dream state will form a collage of information that becomes your own unique dream language.

In my book *Dearly Departed* I explain a simple exercise about how you can program your dream life to give you answers to your questions. I now never, ever, doubt my dreams. They may need some interpreting, but when I receive a prophetic dream—one that is so clear, often in colour, which I can recall in minute detail—I know I need to pay attention. It is spirit inspired!

Sometimes we jam the communication lines between us and spirit. For many people, the constant chatter in our minds, along with the fast pace of our daily activities, inhibits the accessibility of messages being sent from the spirit world. But spirit never gives up, and often dreams are the best way to get through to us. This is why, when we sleep, we are more open in our dream state to receiving premonitions, direction and information that we have subconsciously blocked during our waking state.

So how does spirit talk to us in our dreams?

The language of spirit during our dreams can come in symbols, pictures, words or role-playing. You may see a sinking ship, which is telling you that you're feeling swamped with responsibilities or that something is about to come to an end. It may be indicating that you need to reach out for a life raft in your personal life to stop you from drowning or feeling overwhelmed. Is that life raft a friend, family member or counsellor? Or it may be forewarning you of an event to come that will have a major impact on your life or circumstances.

How can you help this process along?

I strongly recommend everyone keeps a dream diary, whether it's a notebook or a computer file, documenting in detail what you remember and the emotions you felt during the dream experience. This is best done upon waking, while everything is fresh and easy to recall. A prophetic or message dream will often be in colour and be crystal clear. As you collect this information, you will learn from your own set of symbols and dream language and this can assist you in interpreting and understanding your dreams.

Have you ever been to a place and known and felt that you have been there before, or perhaps that you know what's around the corner? Maybe you have astral travelled and visited this place in a flying dream.

Sometimes, for example, you may have a repetitive scenario or person in your dreams. What is it trying to tell you? It was through this exercise that I came to realise that every time I had a dream of Arnold Schwarzenegger, whose role as Terminator was to go back in time to change the future, it was signalling to me that my own future was about to change.

3

REACHING OUT BEYOND THE GRAVE

Every moment of every day those in spirit are watching on and providing guidance when we most need it. For example, the sudden urge to stop what you're doing and call a relative, only to find out that they are ill and unable to remember your phone number; or perhaps for some reason you felt you needed to slow down as you drove over a hill, only to find an accident that you, too, would have been involved in. Whether we take up this guidance is up to us. We have free will.

Our guides come in many shapes and forms. Some you may never have known in this lifetime—they've been selected to nurture and give you guidance based on their level of spirituality. There are also the guides who have an earthly link to you—such as friends or family—those you love in this life.

One of the most remarkable examples of a loved one reaching out from the spirit world happened to my youngest son, Brendan.

Brendan hadn't liked the pace of Sydney. It was too much of a rat race for his liking. So in his early youth he had moved to the tropics; a good three hour plane ride when I visited. He relished the slower paced lifestyle. Now in his twenties, a father to daughter Claira, his weekends were filled with parenting responsibilities.

'Mum, ring me. Pa has just saved me,' were the faint words rebounding in my ear from the message he left on my mobile phone.

It was a flashback moment. Once before I'd heard the same words, felt the same emotions. Could history really repeat itself?

A number of years before, my eldest son Andrew had found himself in a life-threatening situation when a crazed drink-and-drug-affected man took a broken bottle to his throat. Miraculously my father—his grandfather—appeared in spirit and asked Andrew to repeat the words he told him over and over, until the man became subdued and released his hold on the bottle, allowing my son to gain control of the situation.

Unable to contact me at the time, Andrew rang his grandmother, telling her, 'Pa has just saved me.'

Now, fourteen years after my father passed over, I had heard the same words again, this time from Brendan. It chilled me to the bone. Just as I was about to return his call, the phone rang again. It was Brendan, and he had an amazing story to tell me.

Two weeks earlier Brendan had rung to say he and his mate were heading up to the Gulf Country in Far North Queensland to hunt wild game. I felt sick when he told me! A forecast made earlier in the year by my astrologer had highlighted that in the month of November there would be a major issue with one of my children—illness or perhaps a near-death experience. And here we were, the trip was to take place in November.

Brendan laughed when I reminded him of my astrologer's words, assuring me in his carefree Aussie way, 'She'll be right, Mum, no worries. I'll ring you when I get back.'

The Saturday prior to his return I couldn't sleep. I was up all night coughing and worrying. I wondered why I was anxious. Was it because I would miss out on attending my daughter's birthday the following day, as she was living in England? I even got out of bed and had a big drink of water. I was so thirsty, though I didn't know why. I scuffled through the medicine cabinet and found some old cough lozenges. But I still couldn't sleep. If only I had known what I was picking up, or rather, what my body was picking up—it was a premonition unravelling.

I am a psychic, but I don't operate 24/7. I have learned to switch on and off. Like all professions, there is a time to be on duty and a time to be present in the moment with family and friends and for fun. This work is very emotionally demanding and physically draining. In earlier years my psychic radar was always on—I would walk into a shopping centre and feel overwhelmed with the chatter from people's spirit guides. I would feel faint and lose the colour in my face as the energy zappers drained my psychic senses. Over the years I have learned to control my abilities with protection strategies and can easily flip from 'on' to 'off' duty mode, no different from a television remote button waiting to be pressed to activate the television reception.

There are some things we're not meant to know or experience in advance. It's part of the karmic path and lessons on life's journey. Through the curve balls that life throws us, hopefully we come to learn resilience, strength, fortitude and courage as we face our fears and adversities. Many people will rise to the occasion and discover an inner strength they never knew existed. Often, new skills or insights learned in the process can have a major impact on the lives of others. Olivia Newton-John, the great Aussie singer/actor, used her personal experience with breast cancer to found Wellness Centres for medical research, treatment and care for the whole person—body, mind and spirit.

If she had known beforehand what lay in store and was able to change her path, then the Centres she was to eventually found would be non-existent.

The same can be said of my profession as a psychic intuitive. Foremost I'm a mum. My career follows next. I cannot be objective when emotions are involved with those I love and care for. This is why I prefer not to read for family and friends (it's no different from a medical doctor who can become too emotional treating a loved one). My concerns for Brendan's wellbeing on the hunting trip were the same as those any other parent would feel—nothing psychic was at play.

For Brendan, it was the ideal time for the camping trip. The wet season wasn't far off, so it would be his last opportunity for several months to travel on the roads that become inaccessible in the Big Wet. Already the humidity was becoming physically draining, with temperatures up in the high 30s. But for Brendan it would not deter him from the fun of 'going bush' with a friend and their dogs—a good campfire, plenty of food and the occasional beer to finish off a great day's activities. And nowhere else did the stars shine so brightly.

One day, in the late afternoon, the boys needed wild game to feed their dogs. Brendan decided to go into the scrub to see what he could find. He was sure he'd be back before dark, and was armed with his bow and arrows, compass and two-way radio. But he omitted to include one essential item—water.

He had sighted a wild scrub bull and the chase was on. The bull had the advantage as it knew the lie of the land. Brendan just followed, until finally he had to stop to get his bearings. He checked his compass several times to make sure he was on track. The only problem was the bush was becoming denser and denser, and the sun was starting to set. Light was fading fast and he knew he had to hurry back to camp. The two-way radio couldn't get any signals, so he picked up his pace and rushed deeper and deeper into the scrub, looking for the track he had taken. He had to get back. Then, a shock—he realised his compass wasn't working. He had no bearings. He couldn't even see the direction of the sunset. He was lost in the wilderness.

Dingoes were known to be savage in the area and Australia's deadly taipan snake flourished in the saltbush country. The waterholes were dry, waiting for the coming wet season. All that was left were salt flats. There was no fresh water, and Brendan was parched.

As nightfall approached he hurriedly made a fire to keep away the predators. Thirst became an obsession. Uncontrollable coughing led to a choking sensation. Brendan knew he was facing death. His life flashed in front of him. He was prepared to die, but he didn't want to die choking. His urine had turned brown. Knowing this was a sign that his body was shutting down, he had no other option but to drink this life-giving moisture. He had one regret—not seeing his beloved two-year-old daughter Claira prior to his trip.

Brendan made a final gesture by hanging his bow and arrows high in a tree, hoping this would be a sign for the search party to find his body. He lay on the ground next to the fire with his knife in his hand. Should any dingoes approach, at least he had some form of self-defence. Gagging with extreme thirst, he cried as he contemplated his death.

Then he had one last moment of hope. He called out to his grandfather: 'If there's ever a time in my life that I need you, I need you now. I need you to show me the way out of this place. I'm lost. I don't know how to get back to the camp.'

Fatigue overcame him and he fell asleep.

Opening his eyes in the morning, he immediately saw that his bow, which was hanging in the tree, had changed direction. It was now pointing to something on the ground. It was then that Brendan noticed his belt had been removed during the night, and next to it was his knife. Together they lay on the ground in the shape of an arrow. Beside them was his compass, also pointing in the same direction.

What did it mean? Brendan wondered. Could it be that Pa had rearranged everything to point the way to the camp? It had to be a miracle. But how could Brendan be sure?

Before the heat of the day became intolerable, Brendan had to make a life or death decision. For him the choice was obvious. He would place his faith in his grandfather's divine wisdom and follow the direction of the arrows.

As it turned out, Brendan was only a few kilometres from the camp. He was amazed to discover that he was so close to safety. The relief of his mate was clear. He had feared that Brendan had succumbed to a snake bite or that a terrible accident had occurred.

Those in the afterlife do watch over us. They still care about what happens to us and sometimes, just sometimes, when we call out for their help, they can manipulate circumstances to turn our fate around. Brendan's grandfather lived a good life. He gave so much to his family, community and church. He was a soul whose spirit soared to his maker after death where again he would be able to protect, nurture and look upon those he loved and adored.

You, too, can call upon spirits that have passed over to guide and assist you. Be mindful when you call and ask for help that you choose someone whose life was a good example on earth. Personalities do not change when they move to the other side. Therefore, if you call upon a friend who was dishonest, their personality traits of manipulation and cheating may not resonate with your needs. Equally, if you call upon a relative who adored you and had your best interests at heart, you will receive the loving protection or nurturing you require.

When time permits, you may wish to light a candle, say a prayer or visit a place that was significant to you and your special person. You can speak to them in words or in your mind, or write a letter. They see, feel and sense it all.

4

PROTECTION FROM THE SEEN AND UNSEEN

Brendan's story is one of trust. He was guided by a higher power; a supernatural force who saved the day. Yet there are those who have no faith or belief system. Can someone else's prayers or belief system override other people's thoughts and patterns?

Since time began human beings have used talismans, amulets and charms to ward off evil or to bring them good luck. In today's society it's not uncommon to see someone wearing a crucifix, religious symbol, pentagram, Eye of Horus, scarab, crystal or semiprecious stones for the very same reason. Prior to being worn or displayed, many of these spiritual objects would have undergone a cleansing and/or other ritual, followed by a prayer to program or imprint them with a blessing or intention.

It's much like placing a virus protector in your computer—without such a device your computer is open to attack. Your thoughts and those of other people's can imprint both positive and negative energy in any object or place. Have you ever walked into a room or building and it didn't feel right? While at other times, it felt just right? Our subconscious can be a powerful tool or weapon—as Japanese Masaru Emoto was to discover in his research on the effects on water subjected to music, words of intent or prayer. What he observed was that the water's molecular structure went through a radical transformation, which saw changes in shape, size, texture and enhanced beauty. We, too, can adopt the same principles with our spiritual objects.

My mate Henrik's experience with his amulet gave me goosebumps. Tall, blond and robust, Henrik hails from Sweden; his approach to life was very logical and he disregarded anything paranormal. His wife Mai is petite and dark-haired, from a Chinese/Thai background that is full of mysticism, ritual and ancient belief systems.

Mai also has good business sense—while Henrik was away working as an engineer on merchant vessels sailing the waters between Australia and Asia, she was busy creating successful commercial ventures.

For example, Mai started a type of cooperative where she lent seed and land for the locals to grow crops. The proceeds of the harvest after costs were equally divided fifty-fifty, between herself and the growers. Henrik recalled the local money lender feeling the loss of some of her regulars.

Henrik also remembered an occasion when he bought his wife a nice shopping bag he found in a market. She wasn't happy at all.

'You idiot,' she said. 'We make them! Don't you ever listen or look at what I tell or show you?'

While Henrik may not have shared his wife's belief in spiritual matters, he trusted her faith enough to feel comfortable wearing a gold amulet she gave him when they first met. The amulets are very much a cultural tradition in Thailand. They are made from a mixture of ashes from a deceased monk or other holy person and clay, pressed into a small mould and fired. The majority are cast in bronze, but Henrik's wife chose to have his encased in gold. Once complete, the amulets are then subjected to long and intense prayer sessions in the temple, sometimes for several years. They are regarded as sacred charms that bring good luck, peace and protection, and they carry with them distinctive powers of positive energy combined with the good karma of the monks who created them.

Henrik liked to boast that every time he played a friendly game of Yahtzee during a voyage, he always won because of the power and luck of his amulet. However, when he lost his amulet, he noticed that his luck had diminished. Sometimes he won, but so did his opponent—there was nothing but chance involved.

One day, his opponent, who was the ship's first engineer, was working under the floor plates in the engine room and his flashlight illuminated an object in the dark. It was Henrik's amulet! The gold casing had acted as a beacon. Perhaps his luck hadn't left him completely. His mate returned the amulet to Henrik to be once again worn around his neck.

They continued their games of Yahtzee, but they started to notice something odd. When they checked the results from the evening's games, Henrik had won them all. He thought his luck was back, but the next time they played his opponent won all the games. Overall, the wins were even. And no matter how many times they played, his mate won exactly half the games and Henrik won the other half.

'Why had the pattern of luck changed from winning, to losing and then fifty–fifty?' Henrik asked me. 'Could the amulet really have a mind of its own, to allow even distribution of wealth?'

He also pondered whether his wife's thoughts and attitudes to fair trading were imprinted along with the soul of the deceased monk in his amulet. That there shouldn't be an imbalance in wealth—or winnings—and one should not have power or dominion over another.

Henrik believed his good fortune changed when he lost the amulet and, once he had it back, he thought his luck would improve, but instead it reverted to balance between the two players. Was he being taught a lesson in humility? Perhaps he needed to learn that there is more to life than winning; indeed, it's how you play the game—fairly, equally, sharing the goodwill and luck. Did the amulet really possess a power; that of the deceased monk, trying to bestow the lesson of sharing? It was all too spooky for Henrik and his mate—and they decided to stop playing!

If you are considering purchasing an object to provide protection and positivity, allow your intuition to guide you. Are you drawn to a particular colour, shape or design? Hold it in your hand, and ask yourself, 'Does it feel good?' Or perhaps you get a creepy sensation. Ask the seller if the item is suitable to immerse in water. If so, when you get home, dissolve some salt in water and soak the item overnight. This will cleanse any residual negative energy that may have been stored. If you can't place the object in water, you can wave some white sage or smudge stick smoke around it. Smudge sticks are wonderful tools and are considered sacred by the Native American people because of their effective purifying energies. They can be bought at new age shops, and every home should have one. After cleansing your object, hold it in your hand and clearly state your intent. Are you seeking protection, love, harmony or good health? Tell the object what purpose you seek from it—you must be very clear. If you're feeling negative that day, do not try to program your object, as part of your energies will obstruct the goodness you wish to instil.

A Chinese Grand Master gave me two special protective wall hangings imprinted with his powerful energy, to hang in my apartment. Each year I return these to his practice for a 'top-up'. Just like our cars need fuel top-ups and servicing, so do our protective devices. I regularly cleanse my crystals with salt water, smudge the house and myself with a sage stick, and if possible have a saltwater bath or a dip in the ocean. People often say they feel fantastic after swimming in the sea—they don't realise it's the salt that cleanses their aura of any negativity.

You may consider asking a member of the clergy, holy person, monk or shaman to bless your object, too. We all have our own light source; some shine more than others. Can someone's goodness really bring peace, good luck, protection and ward off spirits, ghosts and evil? Spirit shows us that it can.

5

OUT OF BODY EXPERIENCES

Though not everyone does so, we all have the ability to travel out of our bodies. The great mystics and yoga practitioners who are highly skilled in deep meditation are able to have out-of-body experiences at will. Their spirit body separates from the physical body, enabling them to travel to another part of the planet or to other dimensions of time and space including the astral plane—the plane closest to earth.

You don't need to be a mystic or a psychic medium to have such an experience. Everyday people who have no knowledge, skill or understanding of astral travel—or, as some refer to it, flying dreams—have had the same experience while in a deep state of sleep where they find themselves separated from their physical body. Scientific studies indicate that most out-of-body experiences occur when we are falling asleep or coming out of sleep; it's during this state, called REM sleep, that the most vivid dreams occur.

In REM sleep the muscles are immobilised, preventing us from acting out our dreams. Occasionally, this paralysis turns off or remains active while our mind is fully awake and aware of the world. For others, astral travel occurs as a result of a near-death experience, stress, trauma, illness, surgical operation, drug experience, sleep paralysis or perhaps in meditation. Those who have experienced it usually describe a sensation of having left their body and being able to view themselves from above, below or some distance away—it is as though they are the onlooker during the event or experience. In fact, what they are experiencing is the separation of their physical and astral bodies, with their astral body then travelling to the astral plane.

Have you ever been woken from sleep by your body jumping or giving you a sudden jolt? This is believed to be the moment when your two bodies are merging, literally bringing your astral body back into your physical body. It's just like when a plane lands on the tarmac and you feel a sudden jolt as the wheels hit the hard surface. When your astral body rejoins your physical body, you feel the jolt as you are coming back down to earth, too.

When you're in the state of astral travel, your physical body remains where you fell asleep—in bed, on the floor or a chair—while your subtle etheric astral body does the travelling. It may be easier to think of it as your mind travelling.

Many people say they don't dream, let alone remember their dreams, yet we all have them. Those who do recall dreams, especially astral projection dreams, can accurately describe in great detail the scenes, shapes and senses they witnessed while they were out of their body. It is as though we become time machines, moving forwards or backwards or in another dimension or another part of our world. Have you ever been to a previously unvisited place and known and felt that you have been there before? Or perhaps felt that you know what's around an unfamiliar corner? Maybe you have astral travelled and visited this place in a flying dream.

My mum had amazing flying dreams. In one early experience as a young woman Mum dreamed she was in another country. She described in detail a house, its furnishings and what was on the mantelpiece, and that the people were olive-skinned and dark-haired. There had been a death and everyone was crying. The next morning she was sharing her dream with her Spanish neighbour Josie, who lost the colour in her face and became very upset: Mum was describing in great detail Josie's mother's home in Spain.

A day later Josie received a telegram informing her that her mother had passed away—at the exact time Mum had her dream. Maybe Mum's ability to astral travel had, in a strange way, been used as a tool to convey to Josie what had happened, or perhaps it was Josie's mother's spirit using Mum as a vehicle to relay her passing to her daughter in another country.

My friends Mike and Yulanda are both very intuitive, which makes for some interesting experiences. They were living in Bali in 2009 in an upstairs apartment with a closed-in balcony. It was about 1 a.m. and Mike found Yulanda crawling on the floor, crying and trying to put clothes into a suitcase. She was calling out, 'I must get back to Papua,' over and over again. Mike managed to calm her down and get her back into bed. Then, about 2 a.m. they heard three loud taps on the balcony door, but no-one was there. In fact, as Mike explained to me, it was near impossible for anyone to climb up to the balcony from the outside of the building. Soon after, they got a telephone call from Yulanda's sister saying her father, who lived in Papua, had passed away at 2 a.m. Yulanda has no memory of crawling on the floor crying.

I explained to Mike that this was a brilliant example of a flying dream, where Yulanda, in her dream state, connected with the spirit realm which informed her that a loved one was passing. Considering Yulanda's wonderful mystic background, it didn't at all surprise me that her beloved father would come to let her know of his passing.

Mike later told me that it was the custom in Papua for the father's body to be taken back to his family village where he was born, to be buried with his other departed relatives. The family tried digging his grave in three places, but each time the earth collapsed inwards. It was a sign that he wasn't happy with their choice of location for his final resting place. So his brothers talked to him, seeking his advice about where he would be happy to be buried. They only had to dig in one more place and obviously he was pleased, as the digging went well and that's where he lies today.

A few days later, Yulanda's 109-year-old grandmother was found with no breath and no pulse. As her family began to prepare for her funeral, people came to her home to say their last goodbyes and pay their respects. But two days later she woke up—she wasn't dead! Her explanation was that she had gone to say goodbye to her son in the spirit world! Before this episode, Mike had been told by Yulanda's brother that a long time ago his people could leave their body and fly—and it was, indeed, what the grandmother had done. She had used her ability to astral travel to visit the realms of spirit to meet up with and communicate with her son. Mike never doubted their abilities, because over the years he'd personally had some mighty unusual experiences around time and space.

Can everyone astral travel? Could this travel take you even to the other side of the world, to communicate with and assist those who are in danger or to pass on messages from the spirit realm?

Certainly, by heightening your psychic receptors through meditation and learning to ground yourself, you will become more in tune with your subconscious mind, which gives messages while in the dream state. Remember to keep a dream diary and write down your dreams. Think back to when you learned to drive a car: at first, you thought you would never master all the skills required, but over time it became automatic. It's the same with astral travel—it becomes easier as you train your mind and develop your sixth sense. I am totally against using any form of drugs to induce altered states because you're not grounded or emotionally stable in these states, and therefore not able to edit or interpret clearly what you have experienced. Using the dream technique described in my book *Dearly Departed*, you will learn how to program your mind prior to sleep to receive answers to your questions. As you become proficient in this technique, so too your ability to astral travel may well reveal itself.

6

WHEN TIME STANDS STILL

Humans created the concept of time. Our perception of time is just that. In the world of spirit there are no clocks—time is elastic.

Mike felt at home with the supernatural beliefs of Yulanda's family—it made sense to him and he felt open to discuss what he had never discussed with anyone in the West in case they feared he'd gone crazy. He told me about an experience in the early 1990s when he was travelling with his ex-wife and son. They were in a car he was driving uphill on a fast stretch of road, and on the brow of the hill a large truck was overtaking a slow tanker. Mike saw it with only seconds to spare—there was no way of stopping or going around the other vehicles. It seemed that death would be upon them. Then, after a short period of time that Mike said was 'blank' and of which he has no recollection, they were past the truck and still driving, safely. He looked at his wife in disbelief—they should be dead. There was no explanation for what had just happened.

Perhaps Mike had a road angel looking after him, although I have another theory. But before I explain what I think happened to Mike, I want to tell you about another experience associated with travel which he had several years later.

In 2005 Mike was in Lanzarote, a Spanish island, and was about to cross a long straight road. He forgot the golden rule—look both ways—and stepped onto the road just as a double-decker bus rushed by at very high speed. It was so close that Mike could feel the vortex of the wind sucking him in, but from behind he felt an iron force grip him—he likened it to being frozen in time. Miraculously, the bus passed him and he continued across the road unharmed. On this occasion, too, Mike should have been killed.

Both experiences made a lasting impression on Mike—he felt there was something mystical and magical watching over him and his family; a power source greater than he would ever understand.

So what's my theory on what happened to Mike? Was it like *The Twilight Zone* or *The Time Machine*, where the physical is taken into another dimension in time and space—an altered period of earth time? I suspect what really saved Mike was the contract he made before coming back to this life where he was given options to select regarding when he would return to his spiritual home. It is said we have a number of exit points in the physical life where we can choose to pass over. An example would be a near-death experience or, in Mike's case, events that could have easily resulted in his death. Always we have our free will as to whether we go or stay on earth, and the longer we stay the more lessons we can learn. Mike certainly had his fair share of 'near misses'. But why? It was obvious to me that the spirit realm had more earthly learning in store for him.

7

EXIT POINTS

Were Mike's near-misses exit points? Were these events he had foreseen when in the spirit world, where all experiences are scripted prior to action in this life? Were they part of his life contract or karma to be played out again in the cycle here on earth?

As an apprentice to the spirit world I know I will be learning until the day I die—and then even more so on the other side. I don't profess to have all the answers, and of course there are so many theories around karma, life contracts or scripts and exit points. My personal sense of what Mike experienced was that he did, in fact, use up two of his exit points. Some say we have five or even more exit points, opportunities where we could pass away or opt out from this life, such as near-death experiences. I really don't know how many we have, but I would strongly suspect in some people's cases they do have more than one.

EXIT POINTS

Almost all of us can recall an occasion when we met someone for the first time and felt very strongly that we knew each other from somewhere before, but we couldn't identify any connection in this lifetime. I would suggest that your meeting took place on the astral plane or in another lifetime where your souls had a previous encounter and now recognised each other for another earthly interaction. Even if this connection was only fleeting, or at the precise time of a monumental change in either of your lives, it provided energy for healing, perhaps for the past, present or future.

When you pass from one lifetime on earth to the spirit world, the physical life you have left behind is reviewed, along with your past lives. What each life provided for your growth and healing is considered, as well as what you need to experience to achieve spiritual nirvana. Strategic planning is required for your next lifetime and who you will share this experience with. Familiarity is comforting but sometimes stressful depending on the relationship you had with individuals. There are always lessons to learn, so it's not surprising that when you reincarnate you will be intertwined with your spiritual family as you play many different roles during your multiple lifetimes together.

The book by Dr Brian Weiss, *Many Lives, Many Masters*, is a great read and includes wonderful stories of the relationships that people have in their current lives which are continued from their past lives. Don't be surprised if you find, for example, that your child was your parent or partner in a previous life—remember that the soul is eternal and we can meet one another again in many lifetimes.

It is why we often have an instant connection with some children or grandchildren, while others we may love but the close bond is just not there. Their emotional link or pull may be to your partner or another family member. Many parents are ashamed to admit these feelings, but I am here to assure you it is natural. The soul remembers all. Those you are favouring with an intense emotional connection may have been your husband or wife or child in a previous life. The love you shared has endured and has now overflowed into your current life situation. It may help to seek out a qualified past-life therapist to assist you in understanding those feelings and why they are occurring.

In the spirit world, once the script is planned and written, you choose the players, just like making a movie. Who is going to play the hero, the victim, the rescuer, the abuser and the pleaser? Will the character be male, female or animal? Where will it be set—which country and which town? Will you have children, who will they be and which order will they take? Who will be your friends and enemies? What are to be the challenges or goals that will push you to refine your soul in this life to come? Maybe you need to learn self-reliance or confidence? What experiences will best help you achieve your purpose in the next life?

Mike's near-death experiences gave me goosebumps—he lived to tell his stories. But what of those whose near-misses eventually led to their deaths?

The headlines said it all: 'Avalanche victim escaped death only three weeks ago.' Jonathan Morgan, 38, had been involved in an avalanche in New Zealand where one of the party had been buried alive and died. Jonathan lived to tell the story. Then, three weeks later, he was relaying the events of that fatal day to a group of people he would be skiing with the next day. But history repeated itself—Jonathan got into another avalanche, which he tried to ski out of, but something hit him on the head and he tumbled down and was buried in snow. He was found and dug out, but was unconscious and did not respond to the desperate efforts to revive him.

Had Jonathan bargained for extra time? Did he need additional time to put his affairs in order?

I saw a parallel in the short time span between Jonathan's first potential exit point and his death with German tourist Isabel von Jordan who narrowly escaped the Bali bombings in 2002. Her decision to leave the Sari Club an hour before the bomb exploded saved her life. Her friends were not so lucky and were evacuated to the Northern Territory for medical treatment. Isabel's decision to fly to Darwin to visit the wounded would be a fatal choice. Ten days after surviving the Bali bombing, she was taken and killed by a crocodile while swimming in a billabong in Kakadu National Park.

Exit points may present as an illness, a fatal accident, a murder or, for some people who find life so difficult, suicide. Where does healing come about in such serious occurrences in life? Knowledge is power. When you accept that you wrote this script for your own development or for that of others, you can no longer blame someone else or a higher power or God or spirit. It's about accepting that death will come to all. But there's also a positive aspect—that the soul is given a choice, and if they wish they can choose to return to their body to continue until the next exit point.

8

LOVE NEVER DIES

It is said we choose who our parents will be according to the soul lessons we, and they, need during our time on earth and to achieve the thousand and one things we need to do. All this is quite understandable, but there is more to this scenario than meets the eye.

Tahlia was an IVF baby and welcomed to this world as the most precious gift any parent could receive. But in the early months of her life, she was diagnosed with stridor—a noisy windpipe resulting from loose tissue on the larynx. Her doctors said it wasn't uncommon for newborn babies and in time she would grow out of it, so her parents Paul and Joanne settled back to enjoy their beautiful little girl.

During her first year Tahlia had some very bad chest infections, and had to spend a lot of time in the intensive care unit of the local children's hospital. On her second hospital admission, her doctor recommended a bronchial examination, to help her return to full health. For her parents it was an extremely scary and stressful time. They stayed with their sick child around the clock, so one of them was always by her side.

Remarkably, Tahlia could still summon a smile from underneath her oxygen mask. She recovered, only to be diagnosed with an extremely rare condition associated with the main arteries and airways in her windpipe. At the time of her diagnosis, Paul and Joanne didn't realise how serious her illness was, until they were informed that Tahlia would require major surgery as the condition had a 20 per cent mortality rate.

The doctors wanted to wait until Tahlia was well and truly over her chest infections and at her strongest before undergoing surgery. Tahlia was animated as her parents drove her to hospital for the operation. Dressed in her favourite pink pyjamas, she sat in her car seat pointing at the purple flowers on the trees lining the road. Paul carried her into the pre-admission clinic, but soon she was running around the clinic laughing and giggling. As he watched his two-year-old daughter, it was as if nothing was wrong with her; she looked so healthy. But 54 days later he would carry Tahlia from the hospital to the mortuary.

For Paul and Joanne it was an effort just to open their eyes each day. They had lost their only child.

It was at this time Joanne began reading and listening to stories about people with special gifts, and she heard me on the radio one morning. From the radio show Joanne went on to read my books, *Dearly Departed* and *Amazing Encounters with Those Who Have Passed Over*, and this led her to book a Dearly Departed session with me. Was this a coincidence or had Tahlia's spirit helped guide her mum to get the information she needed to join the dots and heal her grief?

On the day of the reading Joanne's parents brought her to my apartment and waited in their car while Joanne had her session. It was an emotional reading for everyone, including me, as Tahlia had only passed away six weeks earlier. I had pondered about what a little child could possibly tell her parents that would ease their heavy burden. However, that day, I learned the power of the psychic traveller, the ability of a spirit to move through space and time to give the most amazing proof that life is indeed eternal.

Tahlia came through so energetically and her message was so clear that Joanne was left in no doubt that this was her beloved little girl speaking to her. The energy needed for a soul in spirit to communicate is great and demanding. At times it is as if communication is cut off between the medium and the deceased loved one, only to return with another burst of enthusiasm—they need their batteries recharged to continue the journey, just as a car does. Many souls bring forth a teacher or another spirit helper to assist with the recharging. They may not be known to those who are living, but are assigned to the soul to give an additional boost of energy so the session can continue. It is for this very reason one must pay close attention to the messages, symbols and emotions given, as a medium can't make a soul stay.

As I sat with Joanne after the session and she enlightened me on Tahlia's history and passing, she pulled out a toy giraffe from her handbag. It was one thing in the reading the little girl had talked about. It was a wonderful moment which reminded me why I love my work so much.

It is indescribably painful to lose anyone, but especially so when it is a young child. Parents are haunted by the knowledge that their little one had such a short stay—that they'll never get the chance to grow up and marry and travel. It is understandable that some parents feel they will never recover from such a loss, as was the case with Paul.

When Joanne got home from her reading, she insisted Paul listen to the audio recording of her session, but initially he couldn't bring himself to do it. Later, Paul admitted that he needed to be by himself to listen to the reading. We all have our own ways of dealing with death. Some choose to share their grief with family and friends because talking seems to honour their beloved's life. Others, like Paul, choose to withdraw, building walls that cannot be penetrated even by those they love. So one morning, when his wife went out with her parents, he decided to listen to the reading.

The beauty of spirit communication is it touches on really crucial details—important to those who are grieving. During Joanne's reading Tahlia told her mother that she was now very much in good health and she had not been damaged. She made a very clear point of telling her mother that her mind was okay, and this was a message that was vital to her parents.

Paul later explained its significance: 'There was a complication during the operation and Tahlia had to be resuscitated to bring her back to life. She had lost oxygen to her brain and there was a concern that she would have brain damage.' For her parents to learn that she hadn't suffered mentally was a massive relief.

Paul then revealed a very personal experience: 'I remember you saying to Joanne that Tahlia was showing you someone cutting themselves and that she didn't want them to do this. No-one knew, but I sat on my back step one night after she died, holding a knife. I just didn't have the courage to kill myself. I knew Tahlia's message was for me.

'There were lots of other things that came out during the reading that only we could have known,' Paul said. 'That's how Joanne and I knew that it really was Tahlia talking to us.'

As is often the case, it took Paul a while to seek communication with his daughter through a medium. This hesitation often frustrates partners and loved ones who've had a reading and want others to understand and embrace the same process of healing. Not all are ready to face their grief. Is there a right time to face such raw emotions? Each individual is unique and the process of working through the death of a loved one comes quickly for some, while for others it may be delayed. There is no right or wrong time. Listening to the recording of my session with Joanne gave Paul great comfort—he now knew his little girl was okay—but there was more. For Paul, his first reading with me would start a journey that would open his heart and mind to the power of the afterlife.

Paul asked for a reading on the first anniversary of Tahlia's death. He recalled that he'd heard me on the radio a few times and his impression was that I always said what I had to say—a comment that made me smile! 'I didn't know what to expect,' he revealed. 'I'll admit to some degree of nerves.'

He arrived at my apartment in the afternoon and I wanted to start our session straightaway as Tahlia had already made contact with me. In fact, she had appeared several days earlier as I lay in bed—she popped onto the pillow next to me and in her hand was a gold coin. For the next few days, Tahlia followed me around my home with a gold coin in her hand.

At first I thought that perhaps the coin was to put in a supermarket trolley because Tahlia told me that she wanted to go shopping and I kept seeing her with gold coins which she was placing into a slot. But during the reading Paul described what I was actually seeing and he knew exactly what his daughter was trying to tell him.

'In my study I keep a coffee mug with her baby photos on it, and inside I place my spare $1 and $2 coins,' he explained. 'Before I went to work each morning, Tahlia would come and sit on my lap and then, as I was going to work, we would take two gold coins from the mug and she would put them into a mirrored bear money box in her room. This was our ritual each morning before I went to work—never on a weekend, only Monday to Friday—and they were never silver coins.'

Paul added that he continued the ritual after Tahlia passed away, and had, in fact, placed two gold coins in her money box that morning before he came to see me. 'Except now we're on to her second money box,' he said, 'a little butterfly.'

Paul and I talked about many things during that reading, but the significance of the gold coins really stood out for both of us. Tahlia was such an amazing little force of energy who had spent days letting me know that she was well and truly keen for her father's reading. Paul later told me, 'I walked outside afterwards, breathing for the first time in many months.' It reminded me how much I love doing what I do because it does help heal broken lives.

It's not uncommon for those in spirit to send such clear messages. They want their loved ones to heal and will supply them with whatever they can to prove they're okay and to encourage those they have left behind to get on with their lives. At another of Paul's readings, Tahlia had told me prior to the session that she wanted three pink candles on the table so her father could blow them out for her birthday. Paul recalled his surprise on seeing them as soon as he walked into my reading room: 'We hadn't talked about it being her third birthday, so I was caught off guard with the three candles—and they were soft pink, her favourite colour.' But, more importantly, Tahlia's candles aided her father's healing. 'They gave me peace,' he said.

Time is different in the afterlife—less frantic. Those in spirit continue to take an interest in our lives long after they've moved on. 'It was on her fourth birthday that our little girl certainly made an effort to ensure her presence was felt,' Paul said.

We had the reading on Thursday but Tahlia had been waiting with me since the previous Saturday, which I later found out was her birthday. I did tell her that it wasn't time for her father's reading yet, but again her will was so strong. When I relayed this to Paul, he laughed and confirmed that, 'She had all the energy of a determined little girl and it makes me smile, as I can picture that insistent look on her face, with her two hands held upright, saying "Why not?"'

This time, Tahlia told me that she wanted four little soft pink candles on my reading room table and that she was, indeed, a big girl now. Once again, she planned to blow out the candles with her father, but Tahlia had another surprise in store.

I had just moved to my new home and hadn't finished unpacking. My cupboards were full of packed boxes where they'd been haphazardly dumped during the move. Tahlia kept insisting that I unpack one of the boxes, so eventually, after much prodding from her, I did. In it, among a jumble of my belongings, I found a little pink butterfly which had been given to me by someone at the radio station. Tahlia was then adamant that she wanted the butterfly on my reading room table for her father's reading. I had no idea why it was so important to her, but as soon as Paul walked in, he recognised the sign.

'Butterflies have always been very important to us,' he explained. 'They are Tahlia's favourite, and even as a baby she was fascinated with them. She could never pronounce the word correctly so they became "butter-Y's". We have many butterflies in our house and in her room.

'A few weeks before the reading, I had purchased three butterflies—identical to the one on the table. It was clear to me that Tahlia knew about the three butterflies.'

During the reading, Tahlia said that she wanted my butterfly to be added to Paul's three, and insisted they be arranged like a train—in a straight line, not a circle. 'She now has the four butterflies in her room, displayed just as she wanted,' Paul told me later. Then he added, 'It struck me that there were four butterflies and that represented her fourth birthday.'

Spirits are wiser than we give them credit for, and as psychic travellers through time and space they make every effort to communicate with those they love. Small children can show a maturity beyond their years, demonstrating the wisdom of an old sage. Sometimes, their calling cards or signs can be subtle yet incredibly poignant, as Paul discovered.

Several years after Tahlia passed over, Paul took on a new job. While he had progressed in his healing after losing his daughter, the change brought up feelings of insecurity. As far as he was concerned, his new role wasn't what he wanted: it was three steps backwards from the senior management role he had previously held, but it would pay the bills. 'Humility is needed before one can go forward again,' were words I had been given at his last reading and he tried to keep them foremost in his mind as he faced this challenge.

On the first morning of Paul's new job, he had a spare half an hour to clean out the desk of his predecessor. What he discovered he found hard to believe. Among the assorted business cards in the drawer was one of my cards. It was my current card with the lilac butterflies on the back. Sharing that morning's experience, Paul said, 'I felt a shiver when I found it and had to look twice at the card to make sure I wasn't seeing things! It made me feel relaxed in the unfamiliar environment I was in.'

I am sure that wise Tahlia had something to do with my business card being left in the drawer as reassurance for her father in his challenging new job. She knew that for him that day would be another hurdle, another emotional roller-coaster. She was making every effort to let him know that although he may not have the physical support he needed, she was sending the support of butterflies from the spirit world—the sign of transformation—as he was transforming on many levels. That simple business card in the corner of the drawer became a symbol of hope for Paul. Even though the job didn't look very promising at first, Paul then knew he was meant to be in that role for whatever reason was to unfold in the future.

Most importantly, he learned that when a loved one passes over—even the littlest of loved ones—we can be assured they are still very much part of our lives: watching, observing, and sending messages and even demands. Love never dies.

9

A VERY SPECIAL BOX

Spirit speaks to us in many ways and places, and sometimes it's most unexpected. I'd always been attracted to Burma. It was like it was part of my soul. When I was in primary school my parents couldn't understand how a young child knew such a country existed, let alone had the desire to visit this faraway place! It was definitely a mission impossible, or was it?

A few years ago I received an email from my friend Jules. Her husband Peter had been transferred and was working in Burma. Burma? Just thinking of the place made me excited! Communication with Jules, who was in Rangoon, was sporadic as internet cafes were rare and emails were highly censored. But finally the dream email arrived: 'Would you like to visit?' Would I ever!

We agreed to meet at Kuala Lumpur International Airport, as Jules and Peter were returning from holidays via Kuala Lumpur and thought I'd feel more comfortable if we travelled from there to

Rangoon together. Jules and I were happy to see each other again and, along with Peter, their child and nanny, we boarded the plane for the two-hour flight to Rangoon.

I had the window seat, so I was able to enjoy the coastline as we flew over Malaysia and Thailand and then into Burma. As the plane started its descent, Jules pointed out the floodplains that would soon become an inland sea with the onset of the monsoon. Suddenly, I got my first glimpse of the tiny gold Buddhist stupas scattered among the rice paddyfields. This really was a dream come true!

Jules had contacted various antique dealers in Rangoon, and she had already found some wonderful antiques and rings that she knew would appeal to me. At one dealer she had seen a very old, lacquered, Buddhist prayer box which she thought would fit well in my reading room—call it intuition or a great eye!—and she had asked the owner to put it aside for me to view.

There was just enough time to freshen up and off we set. It wasn't the type of antique shop you would see in the West; it looked more like a garage full of junk. It was dusty and disorganised, but it housed some unique and unusual treasures—it was like nirvana to me.

As soon as I saw the prayer box, I decided it was coming home with me. It had the most amazing gold, tan and black hand-drawn astrological symbols on the outside, and when I lifted off the lid I found a small removable tray inside. Beneath the tray was a deep cavity that was designed to house the sacred Pali, the gold-coloured Sanskrit calligraphy prayer sheets used by the monks to read and chant their daily prayers in the temples. The dealer also had for sale a stand that would showcase the box and some Pali prayer sheets. Little did I realise the strength and power of these items.

When I got home I held my Burmese prayer box with great reverence and placed it in my reading room. It was a wonderful addition to the room where I saw my clients, and it brought another spiritual dimension to the space. Delicately painted in gold leaf on all sides, it seemed to possess a stillness, a calmness, that surpassed all everyday experiences.

The prayer box had such a beautiful presence it became a sacred part of my spiritual practice. On small pieces of paper I would write a client or a friend's name who was seeking healing, relief or a specific spiritual request, and place the paper on the tray inside the box. Lots of miracles followed, as the box proved to be a vessel of living energy!

The gorgeous Pali prayer sheets, which I'd had framed, were on the wall behind the table where the box was displayed. These, too, had a special energy of love and blessing, benefiting everyone who came into the reading room for a consultation.

I recall one client arriving for her Dearly Departed session and suddenly becoming very emotional as she sat in her chair and observed the Sanskrit prayers hanging on the wall behind me. Chandrika was from a Sri Lankan background and she explained that the person she had come to communicate with was a devout Buddhist who would read and recite those prayers daily. She took the framed Pali sheets as a positive sign that she was indeed at the right place, with the right medium, but there was more I needed to share with her that day.

A VERY SPECIAL BOX

At night, I always pray for the clients who will be arriving for a reading the next day. I pray that spirit will use me to impart the highest wisdom, knowledge and information my clients are seeking. Sometimes the messages are not necessarily what they want to hear, but what they need to know!

The day before Chandrika arrived, I had received in the post a number of very old Thai amulets made from a mix of clay and the ashes of a deceased monk or holy person. It was my intention to place the amulets in the prayer box in the hope that their sacred energy would assist the prayer requests held inside.

I opened the parcel and admired the wonderful amulets. Then a client arrived so I put them down in the lounge room. That night I went off to bed, totally forgetting to place the amulets in their new home.

During the night, I heard an almighty thud in my reading room. I sat up in bed, my heart pounding. Had someone broken in, or did I have a spirit in the house? I walked down the corridor in the dark and, flicking on the light switch of the reading room, I was stunned to see the framed Sanskrit prayers had fallen off the wall and were now standing upright behind the prayer box, while the lid of the box was gently resting on the chair where I do my readings. It was as though someone had been into the room and arranged these objects.

Then it hit me. The amulets were a great power for good and along with the prayer box and the Pali sheets they would be a powerhouse of positive energy. Was it the centuries of prayers over these amulets that gave them their power? Or did the monk's ashes that they contained vibrate to the prayers and chants from the sacred Pali? Were they all wishing to be united? I knew what I had to do. I rushed into the lounge room, collected the amulets and nestled them safely inside the box, then placed the framed prayers on the wall behind them.

The next day, when I saw Chandrika's emotional response to the prayer sheets, I decided to tell her about my mysterious experience. She then revealed she had prayed to her father that night to give her a sign during the reading—something specific to their culture, faith or religion. Putting the two together, it seemed certain that both Chandrika and I had our questions answered.

There exists an energy far greater than we know, where divine timing can be called upon to bring about a chain reaction here on earth. It can be used to send a message or a sign to bring comfort and reassurance from one world to the other. I am sure the arrival of the amulets was timed perfectly in the spiritual realms to be a blessing for Chandrika from her father.

You can create your own prayer box (even a bowl or shoe box will do), and keep it in a special place—it could be in your garden, your room or somewhere that's sacred to you. Choose a spot that's quiet and switch off all phones and other distractions. You might want to play beautiful music, burn some incense or light a special candle. You can use your box for healing and prayers, like I do, writing the names of those in need on small pieces of coloured paper, noting each person's address (if known), their age and the condition that requires healing. I keep these messages in my box for two weeks and then discard. (If you wish to continue praying

A VERY SPECIAL BOX

for the individual, repeat the process again.) Hold or touch the box while thinking good thoughts and/or say a prayer. Be positive and believe that miracles can occur. No prayer is ever in vain, all prayers are heard by spirit.

10

THE GHOST WITH A DEADLY INTENT

I am blessed to have had some interesting travels with my gift and some unexpected adventures with the other side. Dina was the wonderful Filipino nanny who looked after Jules and Peter's child. I got to know Dina during my visits to Rangoon. She adored Jules and Peter's daughter and at night-time I would lay awake in my bed, listening to Dina's beautiful voice as she sang to the little girl until she was asleep.

I couldn't help but notice how very protective Dina was, as if the child was her own. One day I complimented Dina on her dedication to the child, and made an offhand remark, 'I could well imagine you would even die for her.'

To my shock, Dina became somewhat emotional and proceeded to tell me of an incident that explained her dedication—and it was obvious as she recounted her experience that it still shook her to her core.

Back in Manila in the Philippines, Dina was working for a well-known doctor in a very affluent suburb. Her little charge was only eighteen months old. One night Dina awoke to hear the dog barking—it was an unusual bark, more like baying. Then, suddenly, a ghostly woman appeared at the end of Dina's bed. She had short hair and in her hand she held a long bamboo pole. She moved towards Dina with the pole in her hand, making it clear she wanted to kill Dina. The ghost woman then produced a plastic bag, which she forced over Dina's head, trying to suffocate her.

It was only Dina's long fingernails that saved her. Somehow she managed to dig them deep into the plastic, which enabled her to get a strong hold of the bag and pull it off her face. As she gasped for air, with all her might she screamed for the ghost to leave. A sudden stillness and sense of peace followed—the murderous ghost had gone. The terrifying experience totally exhausted Dina and soon afterwards she fell into a deep sleep.

When she woke up the next morning, she immediately recalled what had happened during the night. Her rational mind kicked in, telling her there was no reason why this should or could happen. She accepted she must have had a nightmare.

But when her employer spoke of the disturbed sleep he'd had because of the very unusual barking that lasted for some twenty minutes, Dina started to wonder if her experience had in fact been a dream. She rushed back to her bedroom in search of the plastic bag used to suffocate her. With this she'd have the proof—that the ghost or spirit who had tried to kill her was real. She looked everywhere in her room, but there was no plastic bag to be found.

Sitting on the edge of her bed, she suddenly realised there was one place she hadn't looked—under the bed. Getting down on her knees, she felt sick when she saw the plastic bag. It was ripped, exactly the way she remembered tearing it. The reality of her night's ordeal hit her. This was no nightmare—it had really happened. Dina also realised that the power of this spirit was great. What if it had killed her? Would the next victim be her little charge?

The experience made a deep impression on Dina. Having been in danger, she was now aware of the forces of the dark. They were real and could be dangerous. From that day onwards, she was determined to do all she could to protect those she cared for and loved.

Dina's experience has an important message for us all. There are some supernatural things that are evil. Not all individuals have positive motives or intentions in this life and they don't suddenly become good angels after death. The dark side operates on a lower frequency, as these entities have chosen to turn away from the light and goodness of this world and beyond. They seek out and are attracted to the higher frequency spirits and individuals who radiate light and goodwill. Like a moth is attracted to the light in the dark of night, they derive great pleasure in teasing and tormenting those who are vulnerable. Just like those who bully people here on earth, they become spirit bullies. They get a kick out of intimidating and harming those on the earth plane.

Like Dina, we need to be aware that the more you fear their actions, the more you are open to their attacks. It's like pouring petrol on a fire. I congratulated her on telling the bad energy to leave. If this was to occur again, Dina knew to stand her ground and to command these scary, dark forces to go away, or to call out to her angels for their protection.

I shared with Dina a technique I have used over the years. The important thing to remember in these situations is not to become a shrinking violet, but to summon your strength and light. Together, in loud voices, we rehearsed this command over and over, so it would easily spring to mind if she needed it: 'Be gone—go to the light, you are not welcome here.'

We then started to giggle, hoping no-one else in the house heard us and were wondering what we were doing!

In the busyness of today's societies, we often forget the beauty of a soothing bedtime ritual. Exhausted, we tuck our children into bed and rush away for some time-out ourselves. Sometimes, the simplest small prayer as you're kissing your child goodnight sets in motion stillness, peace and a good night's sleep. I always give thanks and gratitude for the day that has just passed and ask spirit for protection, love and guidance for the night and tomorrow.

11

CLEARING UNWANTED ENERGY

As it turned out, that wasn't my only experience involving Dina and the supernatural. A couple of years later, as I was preparing for my third trip to Rangoon, I received an email from Jules: 'Georgina, we have a problem in my daughter's bedroom—Dina thinks we have a ghost! Dina's prayers and the commands you have given her don't seem to have any impact. Nothing seems to be working. Is there something you can bring on your trip this time that can help resolve this? I'm so scared—as you know, she shares an adjoining bedroom with our daughter.'

I wondered how the authorities would react if they searched my bags to find a smudge stick—dried leaves of white sage bundled together and tied with string.

Rather surprisingly, I breezed through Immigration. However, everywhere I looked there were soldiers with weapons, from machine guns at the airport to rifles in the streets. Their presence was formidable. Everyone was in a hurry; no-one wanted to be stopped. Perhaps it was a fear of been interrogated by the military, or perhaps they were just rushing to catch one of the uncovered table-top vehicles that offered cheap rides. I certainly didn't feel safe at the airport and it was a relief to see the smiling, welcoming face of Jules and Peter's chauffeur.

Even so, I didn't start to relax until we finally arrived at Jules and Peter's home: a colonial mansion protected by high-walled fences topped with curls of razor wire. The two security guards opened the heavy gates and we drove to the front entrance, past the manicured lawns and gardens. I now felt safe. My heavy bags were carried up polished wooden stairs to the top floor where my room was located, right opposite the room where the disruptive ghost seemed to find great delight in playing games.

My hosts were keen for me to get into action with the ghost-busting as soon as I was refreshed and settled, as they felt they couldn't relax until things had returned to normal. Although Jules is very open to what I do, like a lot of people she had never really believed in the concept of ghosts and hauntings until she had a firsthand experience in her own home. Since the ghost had made its presence felt, she'd started questioning her belief system.

Dina explained that for two nights she had been woken at 2 a.m. and 2.15 a.m. to find her television switched on and showing a program on cable TV. This mightn't have been so strange, except the satellite cable wasn't connected and neither was the TV! Sitting up in bed Dina then saw a greyish outline of a woman standing next to the TV. Instantly recalling the chant we had previously practised, she proceeded to recite it in a loud, firm voice. To her relief, the greyish figure disappeared.

However, several nights later, she awoke to the sensation of someone next to her in bed. It was a warm and comforting feeling. Thinking that Jules and Peter's daughter may have hopped into bed with her, she reached out towards the child but was alarmed to find there was no-one present, yet she could see an indent in the sheets where someone had lain. Dina checked to see where her young charge was, only to find her in a deep sleep in her own bed.

The next morning Dina told Jules about the goings-on in the room over several nights. For Dina it was critical that things settle. Memories of the Manila experience were resurfacing and she didn't want to be on high alert all the time. She wanted peace, stillness and safety. And so did Jules and Peter.

Clearly, it was time for me to get to work. Whenever I think about what we did next, it brings a smile to my face! There we were—Jules, Dina, the child and me—walking around the periphery of the two bedrooms, clapping our hands, loud, loud, louder. The child shook her tambourine. We paraded around the rooms three times, repeating the command, 'be gone, be gone, be gone'. If there had been gongs, prayer bowls or tuning forks—or perhaps even a drum—we could have used them, too, as all these instruments produce sound waves that transform the energy of a space, heightening the energy to higher frequencies and purity.

I then lit the smudge stick, which has a smell I love—although it can be quite overbearing if you don't like the smoke residue. I waved the stick in an anticlockwise direction and used my hand to disperse the smoke throughout the room and towards the furnishings, nooks and crannies—anywhere negative energy can be stored or absorbed.

Then it was our turn to be smudged. Each person had the heavy-smelling sage smoke waved throughout their aura—from the top of their head, to the soles of their feet, including arms, palms of hands and legs. The smoke becomes like a magnet, attaching itself to the negative energies. As the smoke dissipates and clears, it takes the negative energy with it. Tests have demonstrated that the smoke of burning sage actually changes the ionisation polarity of the air.

After this we joined our hands together in a circle and spoke aloud that no uninvited visitors from the spirit realms were allowed entry to the house.

Finally, we placed a large bowl of rock salt in a wooden container under each bed to absorb any residual negativity that may have lingered. The salt was to be discarded in the toilet once a week—flushed away from the home, along with any negativity it contained—then replaced, for as long as they felt necessary.

After our spiritual cleansing session, Jules and her family, especially Dina, were hugely relieved that there were no more experiences with the disruptive ghost.

It was always evident to me that there was really nothing to fear from this ghostly energy—it wasn't an evil or mischievous spirit seeking harm, just a lost one. Lost souls seeking guidance or direction sometimes affix themselves to energies of happiness, love and laughter, wishing once again to feel part of a loving family. In these situations, all that's required is a gentle reminder that they need to move on to the light and no longer be earthbound.

12

BEWARE OF WHAT YOU BRING HOME

There is so much more to the afterlife and other worlds than we realise. Sally's family were very superstitious. It was part of their Indian background. When things went wrong, they'd assume it was as a result of something bad they'd done in a previous life. This belief turned out to be more prophetic than Sally realised.

Sally and I first met through my friend Jules, when I did a Dearly Departed reading around her missing father. Two years later I was shocked to learn that her health had deteriorated rapidly. At times Sally would improve, only to be diagnosed with another illness. She'd also had multiple surgeries. She was frequently in hospital, where she regained her strength and determination, only to find her health declining rapidly when she returned home. And throughout the ordeal, she was never free from pain.

There's no two ways about it, Sally had a privileged lifestyle, with maids, chefs, gardeners and a chauffeur at her beck and call. She couldn't understand why fatigue and illness came over her so quickly once she was home. Because her employees did all the household duties, she spent her days watching television, reading, entertaining friends and maintaining links with her charities.

I was mystified when Sally phoned me and revealed what was happening to her, begging me to come for a visit. 'I trust you, Georgina,' she said. 'With your gifts you should be able to uncover the truth.'

I could feel her pain and desperation, but the task seemed huge. I sensed that whatever was happening to Sally, it was something more powerful than I had ever experienced. There had to be a trigger within the home environment that was zapping her energy. I explained to her that whatever it was, it was not dissimilar to a tick living off the blood of an animal, injecting its toxic poisons into the bloodstream and ultimately causing paralysis, then death.

In Sally's case I was sure that something had interfered with the delicate balance of her aura, the energy fields surrounding her body. I explained there are four layers and to imagine herself as an egg. The beautiful golden yoke was her physical body. The white of the egg was her etheric body that supplied her life energy. The shell was her astral body, and governed her passions and emotions. The unseen space surrounding the shell was her mental body, and this reflected her thoughts and beliefs.

There are, in fact, even more layers to the aura, but Sally was becoming somewhat overloaded, so I didn't go into any more detail at the time. Also, I felt strongly from what Sally had told me that she was experiencing interference between her physical and etheric bodies. This left her feeling ungrounded and was ultimately creating her health issues.

Often, we're more aware of what's happening to us than we think. I'm sure we've all said at some stage, 'I just don't feel myself today', or 'I'm beside myself'. What we don't always realise is that our physical body is reacting to the energetic bodies surrounding it. Or, to put it another way, your aura is out of whack.

All living things have an aura. Kirilian photography shows this quite clearly. As Sally is a Christian, I used the examples of religious paintings with haloes and gold and white lights surrounding martyrs, saints and angels. These beautiful paintings capture the radiant energy force—our aura—extending beyond our physical body. Sally was starting to get the picture, but the questions remained: Why was Sally a victim? And what was she a victim of?

As I thought about what had been happening to Sally, I realised it had all the characteristics of a psychic attack. Sally was alarmed when I suggested that she could have a psychic vampire, someone who was draining her of her life energy, in her household. Images of Dracula and scary movies sprang into her mind and she became even more anguished, until I assured her that sometimes an object or an individual may unknowingly possess toxic thoughts of rage, anger, envy, greed or hate. Or there may be residual energy stored in an object that has experienced some trauma or dislocation in the past. I explained, for example, that she might be wearing her favourite aunt's crucifix: if her aunt had it on her when she died in an accident, the trauma would have been absorbed in the crucifix, and the fear, pain and grief would reach out like tentacles, searching for someone's auric field to attach to.

Put simply, Sally's energy had been zapped! I told her she reminded me of a 100-watt light globe that had dropped to 10 watts. This made sense to her, and Sally could now see the correlation between how she felt and the people in her life. We laughed when we compared certain people we knew—there were those who made us feel alive, refreshed and reinvigorated; and those who always left us drained and who we avoided like the plague.

We are all connected to givers and takers in life. Red flags should pop up if someone constantly says, 'I always feel good around you,' yet they leave you feeling drained. What's happening here is that they have, subconsciously or consciously, tapped into your etheric layer, your vitality. I'm sure if you stop to think about this, you know exactly who these people are in your life. Good, bad or indifferent, it really helps to have people sorted out. In your circle of friends, family and work colleagues, who drains you? You might be surprised to discover that you, too, have a psychic vampire in your midst.

With Sally, my psychic radar was honing in on the possibility that one of her beloved artefacts may well hold the key to the source of her ill health and fatigue. If there was an issue, a possible remedy could be some very strong energy cleansing for Sally and her home.

Where to begin? Sally's home was truly amazing—grand beyond belief. While all her artefacts looked fabulous, unless you tuned into them, you had no sense of the vibe they were giving off, the energy created by what had happened to that object in the past. I started tuning into them one by one—the Madonna statue, the crucifix on the wall—and opened up to my sixth sense, asking spirit to show me where the problem might lay. I could sense nothing draining or dark in their energy. Then it suddenly occurred to me that Sally could help speed up this process.

I asked her, 'Sally, is there anything new that I haven't seen before?'

Sally paused for a moment, and then said: 'You know how much I like collecting my art and unusual pieces from abroad. At a charity function, I was fortunate enough to be introduced to a dealer who specialised in supplying Asian antiquities to museums and private collectors all over the world. She'd heard about my interests, so she extended an invitation for a private viewing when the next shipment arrived.

'Everything was stored in this really dark room under her house—a little bit eerie for my liking! Finally, I spotted several really unique pieces that took my fancy. The prices were rather inflated, I thought, so I decided to sleep on it before making my decision, secretly hoping she would offer a discount.

'The next morning my maid woke me, excitedly explaining that at the front door was a special delivery, a large crate with a golden Buddha statue inside. I rushed down the stairs. Inside there was a note: "Try before you buy." It seemed a fair offer. After all, it was the one piece I had been particularly drawn to. It was covered in pure gold.'

When I asked Sally where the statue was now, she explained that a deal had been struck and it took pride of place in 'the piano room', a new extension of the house where they frequently entertained guests. 'It seemed to take on a life of its own there,' she said, adding that the Buddha statue, in its majestic glory, became a real talking point and focus among their guests.

Then Sally went quiet for a moment before continuing: 'Shortly after the Buddha arrived, my staff and I noticed the lights in the room would flicker intensely on and off. The electrician didn't have a clue why this was happening just in that one room. There seemed to be no power surges in the area and all the wiring was perfect.

'I remember it was also around this time that people started commenting on the chill in the air when entering the piano room. I felt it, too. The staff started to avoid cleaning the room and they were reluctant to answer the service bell when summoned there. Among themselves they refer to it as "The Buddha Room" and they say the room feels strange.'

The more Sally talked about the room, the more obvious it became to both of us that the Buddha statue, once a focal point of conversation and admiration, may well have been a centre of negative energy. 'Our guests also experience unusual, uncomfortable sensations, and there seems to be a reluctance to take up invitations if an event is being held in that room,' Sally said. 'So we've started entertaining in the Bali garden just outside the piano room. In our tropical climate that seems to appease everyone, but now our guests aren't inclined to go into that room at all. It's as if a barrier or a curtain has been drawn, forbidding or prohibiting people from entering. It's very strange. And, to be honest, I'm now wondering whether the statue holds some supernatural powers—whether it's bad, or evil, perhaps even cursed?'

This sounded like a distinct possibility. Flickering lights and cold spots are some ways in which spirits will try and grab our attention. They have the ability to manipulate electricity, and I believe they use it to sustain their activities. Spirits feed off the warm energies, resulting in a significant drop in temperature or a cold spot in a room.

The energies were positive as we strolled through the remainder of Sally's house, until we passed over the bridge into the Balinese gardens that led to the entertainment wing. There was a cold chill in the tropical air. Goosebumps were surfacing all over my body. I felt sick in the stomach.

The cool air made me suspect there was a host living off this energy supply. My stomach or solar plexus area has always been my internal radar—it's like the amber light flashing at the traffic lights, drawing one's attention to changing conditions. What was I tapping into?

As a psychic intuitive, my senses can pick up subtle changes that other individuals may not feel. There was no doubt in my mind. The atmosphere had definitely changed. This had to be the place that was causing problems. Then, out of the corner of my eye, I spotted it—the golden Buddha. It was easy to see why Sally had been entranced by its presence. Special exhibition lights had been installed to showcase its beauty. The lights danced on the surface of the Buddha, giving off a golden glow that made it look like it had its own aura. It couldn't have a life force of its own, could it?

As I neared the statue, I picked up a tangible sense of sadness; a feeling of abandonment. The Buddha was no longer experiencing the reverence it would have been used to in its natural setting and temple of origin. Put simply, this sacred statue was dislocated, in a state of void. The energy I was feeling around the Buddha felt stagnant, thick and heavy. Negative energy can have a furry, unpleasant sensation, just like when you haven't brushed your teeth for a while. Was this where Sally's psychic energy was going? I was on alert!

Sally's face flushed and there was a flash of fear in her eyes. 'Is there something you're not telling me?' I asked. 'Did the dealer give you any background history about the Buddha?'

Her response was a shock. 'These Buddhas she buys, I feel ashamed to say, are sold on the black market,' she admitted. Sally explained how they were stolen from ancient Buddhist temples that had been protected for centuries and revered by the monks whose ritual prayers, incantations and meditations would have permeated the very essence of each Buddha with energies so pure of intent that they are, indeed, the 'holy of holies'. 'It was why I felt I needed to have one,' she added. 'It was a piece of perfection.'

Sometimes it's hard to tell clients the truth, but Sally would never get better if I didn't level with her, as she really didn't know what she'd set in place. 'Sally, how would you feel if someone stole the cross from the Holy Communion table in your church with the intention to sell it for profit on the black market? There's no difference. It's the same. It's sacrilegious.'

Sally looked uncomfortable, but she needed to get things off her chest. 'Georgina, I fear there's worse to tell you,' she went on. 'At the exchange point between the looters and traders, a gunfight ensued around my stolen Buddha and one of the looters was shot and killed.'

For one moment I thought I was part of a movie script. I needed to remind myself that what I was hearing was, in fact, very real. Before I could respond, Sally was able to see for herself what had happened.

'Oh my God, the reality of this is enormous,' she said, on the verge of tears. 'I have in my possession a sacred object that has been uprooted from its blessed surroundings, only to be tainted with murder. And it's true; I possess a stolen antiquity that is very sacred to the monks and their people. I feel so overwhelmed that I'm a party to this awful situation. I've broken karmic laws. I feel I'm doomed. Is my illness my punishment for taking the Buddha into my home?'

'I think we have uncovered your psychic vampire,' I replied sadly. I then told Sally that the residual energy or the imprinting of the tragic circumstances of the theft of the Buddha had created an energetic disturbance. 'It may be that the murdered person's fears, pain and retributional energies seeking revenge have been impacting you, or the displaced energy created by the theft of the Buddha itself.'

We may never know the full story of what happened to Sally's Buddha statue in transit and why the energies were so draining, but one thing was certain—the situation needed to be fixed and quickly.

It was Sally's husband who bravely sought out the assistance of the monks from the local Buddhist temple. Confessing their plight, they begged the monks to help find a solution. Sally later sent me an email, telling me of the events that unfolded following this meeting.

'The monks agreed to come and offer prayers,' she wrote. 'They realised immediately on seeing it that the statue was not from their country, and I confessed that it was indeed from another Asian country. They placed themselves around the Buddha in a circle formation, and they lit and placed a large number of candles around the statue. A friend explained to me the ritual use of lit candles gives the monks a visual point to focus their energy, as well as ingesting and releasing stored negative energy. Then the monks started to chant, and chant, and chant. After what seemed a long time, the candles suddenly all shattered, splattering and exploding simultaneously. I was then told, "It's over. You can keep the Buddha or give it to a temple."'

Many years have elapsed and the Buddha still resides in Sally's 'Buddha room', but I am pleased to report her home is again full of tranquillity. Sally's health has flourished and there are no unusual paranormal activities.

Unfortunately, though, the dealer has since been diagnosed with an incurable disease that will ultimately lead to an early death. The date of the first appearance of her symptoms was traced back to when she started trading in stolen antiquities. There is always a price to pay when your life is not aligned with good intent. One can only imagine how many psychic vampires she has living at her house.

We can all learn from Sally's experience—any of us can be unexpectedly influenced by objects we inherit, buy at markets, or receive as gifts from family and friends. Before placing them in our homes or wearing them, they also need to undergo a cleansing of any negative residual energy. I always smudge myself with sage after I visit museums or places where there are sacred objects as they, too, can hold memories or energies from the past. It is never too late to smudge your home, your possessions and yourself. It is no different than spring cleaning, but it's best to do this at least once a month to maximise purer vibrations.

13

SERIOUSLY BAD VIBES

I am often asked about curses and sorcery in the spirit world. People want to know if evil exists in other realms and if there's anything they can do to protect themselves from negative energies. My answer is that good and evil are everywhere, as the following story proves.

I was in Malaysia staying with my friends Fiona and David, when I heard from one of my clients there. 'I'm planning a dinner party just for you—recipes from my homeland of Sri Lanka—I can hardly wait to catch up with you again! Let's say 8 p.m. tomorrow night?' read the text from Dayani.

It sounded lovely, though I sensed the reason for the invitation wasn't strictly for me to enjoy Dayani's hospitality or a great home-cooked meal. In my line of work I often find there's no such thing as a free meal! Usually the talk at the dinner table gets around to me being asked to read for friends sitting alongside me or being invited to return another day for a consultation. But I love socialising as much as anyone, so of course I accepted.

It would be a chance to meet new and interesting people and sample different cuisine. Although I was assured that the Sri Lankan food would be 'mild', I was still somewhat nervous as Dayani served her homemade feast—I'm not good with very spicy food! My instincts were correct as beads of perspiration turned to a slow trickle, and then a flood, down my severely reddened face—much to the amusement of my friends Fiona and David, and the horror of my hosts Dayani and her husband Sunil. At least the conversation centred on my inabilities rather than my abilities!

But that diversion didn't last for too long because shortly after we finished eating, Dayani wanted to get my opinion on something that had occurred many months before—something she had only shared with her husband and a few household staff.

Dayani explained that she had found the strangest object in her front yard—a lime that had sharp nails embedded into its flesh, so it resembled a weird porcupine. She'd never seen anything like it before. She picked it up and inspected it carefully, all the while thinking how odd it was to find it in front of her house. At first she wondered if her children had made it at preschool, or if a neighbourhood child had thrown it over the fence, but then she thought it didn't look at all like a craft project or something a child would fashion out of interest. The nails were sharp and could easily have damaged a child's soft little fingers. Besides, it was so unappealing and ugly, so sinister.

In the end, she didn't bother to ask her children whether they'd made it. She didn't fancy seeing it sitting on one of their bedroom shelves anyway. It went into the garbage, where she thought it belonged.

About a week later Dayani started to feel exhausted, as though she was coming down with the flu. Her doctor recommended that she rest and the fatigue would pass, but it never went away—she could only plan a day at a time. Then, several months later, she found a lump in her breast and was diagnosed with a very aggressive form of breast cancer that would require radical surgery, and chemotherapy to follow.

While Dayani endured all the stress and pressure of her ill health, she kept seeing flashes of the nail-covered lime and a chill seemed to go right through her body. She started to think that perhaps the object had been cursed but then dismissed it as superstition. Maybe the timing of finding the lime was just coincidence. But, in hindsight, there had been a number of other disruptions in her family's life: they had lost a considerable amount of money on the stock market and her husband lost a major contract at work.

'So, what do you think, Georgina?' Dayani asked. 'Could the lime have had something to do with our bad luck?'

Within my being, it sounded and felt like this was an act of black magic. My psychic radar sensed that it was the work of a sorcerer and that jealousy was the root of the problem.

I asked Dayani and Sunil whether there had been a falling out with family, friends or associates prior to this, or if they had lost a significant person in their lives. They both looked at me in disbelief mixed with realisation. Yes, they explained, there had been a terrible rift between Dayani and another woman, someone who had been very close and dear to her. But Dayani had uncovered that the friendship was false and much undermining had been happening behind her back. This led to a confrontation during which the woman stormed out.

Dayani said it boiled down to jealously, spite and greed. As she spoke, it felt as though a knife had gone through my head. I was picking up the lower frequency intent of this woman: she wanted 'payback' for what had been uncovered and what she had lost. This had to be the source of their trouble.

Although I had little knowledge of their culture, it is commonly known that sorcery is practised in Sri Lanka. I was sure there existed underlying similarities with other cultures around spells or 'contagious magic'. I told Dayani and Sunil that I would need to do some research, then let them know what I discovered. I suggested it would be a cup of tea at my next visit, not a traditional Sri Lankan meal, which made them both laugh.

Reading Isabelle Nabokov, who studies and writes about Tamil religion, rituals and culture, my suspicions were supported. A Tamil sorcerer operates on the principle that an affliction can be transmitted by physical contact. Known as a 'vaipu' or 'deposit', the spells involved infusing certain organic substances and metals—such as eggs, copper foil and, yes, limes!—with sickness and then secretly placing them in the houses of the victims or at a nearby crossroad. When the human target comes into contact with the object, as Dayani did, they absorb the malevolent power of that object. As the object begins to rot, decay or rust, everything the victim owns in the form of wealth and health deteriorates. And wasn't this exactly what had occurred for Dayani and her family?

The good news was that the curse or spell would only last for a limited time. However, despite the short time span, the damage to Dayani's health and her family's financial status had been great.

Over the following weeks, Dayani and her family pursued their own investigations around the woman they felt may have consulted a sorcerer. Although their findings were never conclusive, it was confirmed that there still existed an active community of those who sought the assistance of sorcerers. The sorcerers themselves kept a low profile, to avoid being discovered and asked to leave the country. What Dayani and her family learned was enough to persuade them that they had been, in fact, the target of black magic.

Dayani had access to the best medical treatment available, and Sunil had a strong team of financial advisers behind him, so their priority now was to concentrate on banishing the spell and purifying themselves, their family and their home.

Although the family were not of Hindu faith, they had a meeting with a Hindu priest at his temple, who agreed to perform a number of rituals and prayers to intercede on their behalf. As part of the cleansing and purifying process, they had to take bottles of sacred cow's urine from the temple and sprinkle it around the periphery of the grounds and inside their home. I was a little taken aback when I heard about this, but I was assured that, in Hindu belief, the cow's urine is used in sacred rituals—and has wonderful disinfectant qualities as well!

I've since heard from Fiona and David that Dayani and her family are now healthy, financially secure and as happy as can be. Did the prayers and rituals banish the spell, or had the spell lost its potency as time moved on? Fiona felt that Dayani didn't want to know—all that mattered to her was that she was free of the curse. However, Dayani did learn a lesson from this experience: that the old ways of her country regarding black magic and sorcery are still practised today and one should never let down one's guard. She will always remain vigilant in protecting her family from the darker forces, even if it means consulting a different faith to find the answers.

We, too, can be exposed to toxic thoughts or bad vibes coming our way when there is a falling out with family, friends or associates. Be very much aware if, after such an experience, you feel drained or exhausted or that something just doesn't seem right. A plunge, head and all, in the ocean will allow the salt to cleanse your aura, or you can smudge yourself with a sage stick, or visit an energy worker who specialises in cleansing negativity—these techniques can aid a speedy recovery.

14

A MESSAGE IN THE MIRROR

I love the unusual, and perhaps some would say my career is exactly that! As a small child, I'd collect bits and pieces I'd find at the beach or in the bush, or swapped with kids at school, and hide them in my wardrobe because my mum couldn't stand clutter. I remember her all-too-familiar words, 'Gina, why have you put more junk in your wardrobe?' But to me it was treasure. It felt good to hold them in my hand and it felt good to sleep in a room that held my discoveries. As I grew older I became more fascinated with history and artefacts. I realise they also helped me tap into the energy of the past.

My love of stones, crystals and shells grew to collecting old bottles—I had flashes of who held them, what the people looked like and what the bottles were used for. As my sixth sense heightened and I began to travel the world, the search for unusual pieces and the stories they held became an obsession. I was able to hear things clearly as well as see them.

In the West we have to work a lot harder at our natural intuitive abilities because they shut down so early. But people from indigenous cultures have kept and nurtured their natural-born abilities of intuition—it helps their survival. They're still able to communicate telepathically with the living and also with those who have departed. Using their minds and their rituals, they can send thoughts and messages just like we might send an email or text or make a phone call. But while we need a satellite or cables for our messages to reach their destination, their communications are transmitted out into the ether in energy waves. Because almost everyone has strong psychic abilities, the link is picked up and the message or vision received.

Latoya, my granddaughter Claira's mum, has Indigenous roots, and has had a number of experiences with her own mother sending her telepathic messages to phone her. At one time there had been a falling out between the two of them and Latoya's mum called upon her deceased mother to go to Latoya, who lived hundreds of kilometres away, and get her to contact her. She chanted the request over and over. That same day Latoya was brushing her hair in front of the mirror when she was shocked to suddenly see her grandmother in the mirror's reflection. Immediately fearing that her grandmother's spirit had come to tell her of a death in the family, Latoya rang her mother—just as her mother had requested.

With every win there is a loss. With the advancement of technology, we have everything at our fingertips—or do we? The fast-paced lives we lead have reduced our ability to listen to our inner guidance system—that gut feeling that something doesn't feel right, or that wee quiet voice in your head telling you to call your friend because they need you. We're just too busy to take notice of our natural intuitive abilities, which are genetically programmed for our survival and there to help in everyday life. Our lifestyles have become addicted to technology. But if for some reason technology failed, what do you have to fall back on?

Want to reconnect with your intuitive side? Be still! Busyness is deafness to the spirit world. You don't need to be a great meditator. All you need to learn is to be present in the moment. A little technique I use is to close my eyes, take some deep breaths, and then let my hearing extend beyond the room. What can I hear? Birds, traffic, voices? Acknowledge in your mind what you are hearing, then gradually switch off from these distractions, bringing your hearing inwards—back into the room, back to you, just as if you had activated the switch-off mode. With practice this stillness will come quickly, allowing you access to your higher wisdom.

15

GONE BUT NOT FORGOTTEN

I love my work because every reading is like a new journey, which teaches me more about life in spirit and on earth. I have a little ritual where I practise my stillness exercise to prepare for my sessions. An hour before a client arrives, I go into my reading room to light the candle that I've selected, meditate and invite those wishing to be reunited with my client to come through. Should they come through there and then, I make notes to share with the client at the end of the session.

I don't discuss these notes at the beginning of a session as I don't want the client to reveal any specific details about their deceased loved one that may colour my thoughts and feedback. I want strong, definite proof of spirit communication without any prodding or the client providing unnecessary information that could be deemed as me fishing for clues.

For readings, those in spirit cross time zones, from their dimension to ours, in great anticipation of the forthcoming meeting. As a medium, I'm the bridge that joins these two worlds together; I become the conduit of their emotions and physical health prior to their passing, along with the messages they want to give to their beloveds at that encounter.

I'll never forget the intense and excruciating pain in the back of my head as I prepared for Karen's reading. It was my first reading of the day, a Dearly Departed session, and with less than an hour before the appointment I sat down to meditate, hoping the pain would ease.

The previous night I had replaced the scented candles in my reading room with the purple aromatherapy tealight candles that I love, to enhance the spiritual essence and connection between the client and their beloved. I had placed a similar rose pink candle, representing love, in a little bag for Karen to take home to light in remembrance of her session.

As soon as I began my meditation, a woman came through. She was an older woman and connected through the father's side to a young man who had passed. She showed me that she was the spirit force who took the young man over to the other side at the time of his passing. No-one takes the journey to the other side alone. Always, there is someone to accompany the person and to make the transition smooth from this plane to the next. In many cases it is a deceased relative who becomes the spirit guide. There was so much love in this woman's heart.

Then she said, 'Gladys Knight and the Pips.' I underlined on my notepaper: 'Gladys, Knight, Pips'. It may sound strange but, having worked in radio and print for the last eleven years, I find that spirits often choose words from songs or movies to get their messages across to me in the quickest form. It's much like when you're in a foreign country and you don't understand the language, but through facial expressions and hand gestures you get the message.

It was then I started to feel unwell. I made several more notes about a cake, then retreated to the lounge. The meditation wasn't working and now I had the most severe case of gastric reflux. I didn't know if I was up to the session—my head and stomach were in a bad state.

However, I had to do something, as Karen would be arriving shortly. So I dosed myself up on painkillers and indigestion tablets, and applied lavender oil at the nape of my neck, then trusted that I had already made a connection to Karen's dearly departeds and the link would not be broken.

Suddenly, I felt the young man in spirit prod me to change the pink candle for Karen to a blue candle. As simple as it sounds, that was actually a challenge because I didn't recall having any blue tealight candles. Still, I went through my drawer where I keep my candles. There was a wealth of colours, but no blue, then eventually I found one, just one. Gee! This young man must have known it was there—spirit is grand.

When Karen walked out of the elevator, her small frame seemed out of balance with the large overnight bag she was carrying. I could see the suffering in her eyes and felt an intense pain in her heart as I tuned into her energies. The pain went right through my own heart, like a sword cutting me into tiny pieces. Once she was settled in my reading room, I explained how readings are conducted. She had come prepared, having previously read my book *Dearly Departed*.

I pointed to the notes in front of me, which I had taken at the time of the meditation, and explained that I would go over them with her when the session had finished. She was welcome to take them home (if she could understand my scribble, that is), along with the blue tealight candle.

Although not necessary, I do suggest that clients bring along a photo or an item that belonged to their deceased beloved, if they wish to. These are not for me to study; they are placed on the table in memory of their loved one. Sometimes when the client may be very uptight and tense, I am able to use the residual energy from the item or photo as a link to tap into the spirit world and communicate with their beloved—much like a sniffer dog is used by police to follow the trail of a missing person. Karen pulled a homemade quilt out of the overnight bag and laid it on my lap. She also handed me a photo of a good-looking young man. She said his name was Daniel, but he was affectionately called Dan. He was her son, and was 27 at the time of his passing, which happened six months prior.

Readings flow so quickly. Although I record them for each client, I usually only remember snippets—after all, the information and messages are for them, not for me. So I'm able to share this story with you because of the great generosity of Karen and her family, who have since provided me with information about important aspects of the reading.

As the reading commenced, the woman who had previously connected with me came forward immediately, bringing with her Karen's son, Dan. I told Karen that the woman was older and connected to her father's side of the family, then decided to share the reference to Gladys Knight and the Pips which I'd written on my notes. At first Karen wasn't sure who the woman was, but as soon as I said 'Gladys Knight', Karen knew.

'I thought of my nan, my dad's mum,' she said later, 'as she lived in Knight Street at Arncliffe. Nan helped me greatly while she was alive. In 1973 I was sixteen and pregnant and sent to an unmarried mothers' home before I adopted out my daughter. Nan would come to visit me twice a week, whereas my parents would only come twice a month.'

Then, as the session progressed, a man appeared next to Dan. He was stern, and was showing Dan how to chop wood. To be able to do this, he said, Dan needed to be strong, fit and in control of his body; it was about discipline as well as physical exercise. I relayed this to Karen, who explained that her mother's father and her four brothers were all wood choppers who competed at the Sydney Royal Easter Show. Karen added that the description of the man being stern confirmed that it was her grandfather: 'He was born in 1887 and life was more about work than play.'

During the session Dan was keen to show his family he was regularly connecting from his world to theirs and taking an interest in what they did. He showed me that he cuddled up to his mother at night, and referred to the Beatles song 'A Hard Day's Night', because he felt that her emotions were hidden during the day but at night-time they came to the surface. This really gelled for Karen who said: 'I have felt this more or less from the time he passed. I regularly wake up between 2.30 a.m. and 3.30 a.m. and can't go back to sleep. Last week, as I was just waking, I heard two loud kisses and felt air on my cheek. I said, "Thanks, Dan."'

It was a lovely session. Dan showed me how he stroked the hair of a younger woman. To her, the sensation was like having a spider web in her hair that she couldn't remove. When I told Karen that it was Dan's fingers communicating his love to this young woman, Karen smiled in recognition and confirmed: 'Georgie, who was Dan's girlfriend, has said that she is continually touching her hair because she feels there is something on her hair.'

Our dearly departeds are very resourceful in getting through to us. Dan showed me how he would use a particular smell to get the attention of an older man whose heart was shattered from his death. This man didn't talk much about what happened, but Dan knew the smell would trigger memories of him. Karen knew exactly who Dan was referring to—his father.

Karen told me, 'For about a month or so after Dan passed, Andrew would be first home in the afternoon and he said he could continually smell Dan but found no comfort in it.' However, Karen said that, after the reading, her husband found great comfort and healing from the smell: he now knew that it was a sign that his son was still with him, and he embraced it.

Some things never change for those on the other side. When I made my notes before the session, the young man who turned out to be Dan was insistent that he still wanted a birthday cake even though he'd passed over. During the reading he repeated the message and was very determined that this was to occur. Trying to relieve his mother of the pain and anguish of having a birthday cake for her departed son, I said perhaps a cupcake would do. Suddenly, Dan became very animated: he demanded a big cake, said he would have the whole lot, showed me much laughter and happiness, then made a remark about drinking alcohol. It seemed a bit strange to me, but Karen understood Dan's message.

She explained: 'Dan was a twin to Josh. When Dan passed, one of Josh's first comments was that for the first time in his life he felt alone. Then a couple of seconds later, to ease the moment, he said, "But I get double presents now." I'm sure that Dan was saying, "Give Josh my present, but I still want a cake!" We have a photo of the twins' second birthday with them standing in front of a cake. Dan's hand is on his belly and his look says, "Give it to me!" We also have a photo of Dan, in Greece in 2007, holding a beer in a stein with the same look on his face, which we always laughed about.'

When a beloved comes through in a reading to communicate with their loved ones, there is healing—not just for those who have departed, but for those who are still grieving and connected to their loss. Dan expressed that he was angry with himself that he hadn't listened to the warning signs leading up to his death. On passing, he was shown in the spirit world that his agreement to return as a twin was that he would pass in his 29th year, but his exit point came slightly earlier at 27.

It's this level of detail that brings great comfort to those who are left behind, as Karen later revealed, recollecting the events around

Dan's death: 'We woke up to find him at the door. Initially we thought he was just unconscious, but he had already passed away. There was vomit in his mouth and on the side of the house where he had walked down the driveway. We didn't know what had happened. We found out the next day at the autopsy that he had a brain tumour, which was benign, and his lungs were bad. Smoking for twelve years would only have caused a quarter of the damage. I have said many times over the past couple of months that if Dan had to pass away, he probably did us—and himself—a favour by passing so quickly. I have found great comfort in knowing he had an abdominal aneurysm, which causes instant death. Then, learning that he would only have been here for another two years was even more comforting; if he'd passed away at 29, he would have been very sick by then and our emotions over those two years would have been so up and down once he had been diagnosed.'

Dan was adamant that in 2013 they would know the answer to why he had died, and a door could be closed to his passing. This information was also reassuring to Karen. 'Dan passed on July 10, 2011,' she explained. 'We were told that it could take up to eighteen months until we had a true cause of his death—this clearly puts it into 2013.'

As Dan's energies started to fade, he called out, 'Love ya'. Then he quite clearly showed me the year's calendar, and Easter. He said that he was going camping and would make sure he raced them to get there first. I didn't know what he meant but this detail again confirmed to Karen that her son was very much alive in the world of spirit.

'That's so accurate,' she said. 'His father and his brothers, Josh and Ben, had planned to do the Inca Trail last Easter but it was too late by the time they got around to booking. So they've booked the trip for this year instead and they fly out on Easter Monday. It is, indeed, comforting to know that Dan will be with them, racing them up the trail.'

Well, Dan's dad Andrew, his brother Ben and his twin brother Josh did indeed connect with Dan on the Inca trail. The three men were in Cuzco, Peru, the day before commencing their trek when a street vendor tried to sell some of his goods. They had everything they needed but the man persisted, telling them where to locate his shop and that his name was Daniel. Yes, Daniel! They knew there and then that this was a sign from Dan, who was letting them know that he was with them.

During the trek, one night both Andrew and Ben had vivid dreams about Dan. Comparing their experiences the next morning, they both felt the same—it was like they were greeting Dan after he had returned from a long holiday. Ben even went so far as telling his mother, 'Mum, it was full-on gay. We were hugging each other like we had been apart for a really long time', and at that stage Dan had only passed nine months earlier.

Being able to link two dimensions and time zones together is a gift I never take for granted. In the years I've done this work I've seen countless clients move forward with their grief, sadness and hopelessness to a state of acceptance that life doesn't finish at physical death, that their beloveds are still very much involved in their lives. These sessions also bring healing for those on the other side as they are able to express their desires and feelings to the loved ones they left behind. It gives us hope that memories and new experiences can still be felt, enjoyed and shared with all those we love, both here on earth and beyond.

16

UNWELCOME TOUCH

Mary and I are related through my granddaughter Claira. In one of my trips to see Claira, Mary and I had an interesting conversation. She told me her own grandfather had the ability to sing people to death even when they were islands away. The upside was that her grandmother was the village healer. It was fascinating to hear how Mary's people, who are of Torres Strait Islands heritage, were careful to avoid 'bad luck' or 'evil ways'. She then shared a recent experience she had with dark forces, which I found both intriguing and disturbing.

Mary thought she'd found a bargain painting at the local thrift shop. It was a painting of a hand, and it was colourful, original and entrancing—she had to have it! Having a love for the unusual, she knew just the place at home where she would hang her new piece of art, and perhaps over time she would be able to build a collection.

She placed 'the hand' in the lounge room on the wall facing the front entrance of the house. That meant the painting literally was 'in your face' as you walked through the door. Visitors immediately saw it and everyone commented that it was unusual and strange. There was something else they all agreed on—it seemed to have a magnetic pull that drew them to come closer, observe and even reach out and touch the hand. It was most odd, as those who did touch the painting felt creepy, uneasy and dirty.

Shortly after the painting was hung, there were noticeable changes in the household. Things started breaking frequently. People were more tense and on edge. Arguments seemed to escalate where there had once been congeniality. In the eating and television area, where the family and friends tended to congregate, there seemed to be a chill upon entering the room. It didn't have that warm, inviting feeling that had once made people want to visit and stay and socialise.

Mary also had some weird experiences. At times, she felt there was someone watching her over her shoulder, but when she turned around there was no-one there. She started to think she was losing the plot.

Then she started to observe slow changes in the painting. The hand started to bleed, like the way lipstick does when it goes into the lines around your lips. At first, tiny little lines appeared, but gradually the lines became thicker, resembling drops of blood leaking from the hand. It wasn't just Mary who noticed the changes. Her partner and teenage children all witnessed the changes, too. The painting seemed to possess a life force of its own.

Memories were resurfacing of the powers of the witch doctors or sorcerers back home in the islands. Had she unwittingly brought a bad omen into her home?

One day Mary's three-year-old daughter rushed into her bedroom, crying hysterically. Her daughter said someone had pulled her hair, and Mary could see that her usually neat ponytail was now pointing to one side. Mary asked her daughter who pulled her hair, but she didn't know as she hadn't seen anyone do it. It just happened, her daughter said. Mary initially thought one of the other kids had pulled it, but they were all at school and there was no-one else at home. Even the back and front doors were locked, so there was no way anyone could have entered the house.

All Mary could conclude was that the painting had a power that was being unleashed in her home. It had to go! But there was no way she was touching it. It needed the power of a man to dispose of it. I felt for her son when she told him what she wanted him to do. He would be the one to take the painting off the wall and throw it on the council collection pile on the street in front of their house. She knew the garbage collectors would be around in a day or two and the painting would be gone.

As soon as her son removed the painting, there seemed a freshness in the air. A calmness seemed to be restored to the home.

When Mary recounted this story to me, I couldn't help but think that perhaps it was her own hyperactivity that had changed the energy frequency of her home and that once her fears were put aside she was able to calm down. But then I couldn't explain how the hand changed and dripped blood. I had very little knowledge about her cultural background, but I did know there existed 'contagious magic', magic that could be transferred, affecting a person through something that was once connected to another.

I had seen and felt a transference of energy in jewellery that clients had bought from antique shops, especially from deceased estates, or in jewellery they had inherited. I've seen how the previous wearer's energies and health conditions became part of the new wearer's energy field. Some people became melancholy, more angry or developed a funny habit. It all seemed to start from the moment they wore the newly acquired piece.

When I do a reading, I can feel and read this kind of energy transference when I tap into a person's energy bank. That's why I always insist that the item I hold for psychometry—to help tap into the owner's energies, creating a link between them and myself—has not been worn by anyone else, because I can pick up the residual energy of the other people and there would be a mixed reading of the client's energy and that of the previous wearer's.

I felt that Mary's experience was a case of contagious magic. The painting had been infused with a spell or curse from the previous owner that transferred to whoever possessed it. On reflection, Mary felt strongly the painting had been cursed and was glad it had gone from her home.

As we talked, a vision flashed in my mind—the painting, tossed out for the council collection, was not destroyed and in fact went into the hands of another. I could only hope wisdom prevailed and the person who fell in love with the painting eventually uncovered the truth and destroyed it, thus bringing a halt to the darkness it contained. But if it wasn't destroyed—and this is what worried me—who would become the hand's next victim?

Yes, there does exist both good and evil. Just as we pray for healing and wellbeing at a higher frequency level or wear talismans for protection, others have the power to infuse negativity and lower frequency energy into objects. So buyer beware! A good tip when buying anything, or when moving to a new residence or even staying somewhere on a holiday, is to smudge the object or area with a sage stick to dispel any negativity. When you do this, you will clear away any residual energy stored in the object or place. It's like starting with a fresh slate—clean and purified.

17

DARING TO DO THE IMPOSSIBLE

Walking between worlds lands me in some unexpected places. Sixteen years ago an elderly Scottish male clairvoyant told my mother, 'Someone you know will travel to Rhodesia; they will see elephants.' We had a chuckle at the time. There were no plans for anyone in our family to travel to Africa.

I have since learned the power of being a long-range forecaster. Never doubt the ability of spirit to manifest predictions through the mouths of those gifted with the sight.

Rhodesia was well and truly forgotten when I had a wonderful invitation to join my friend Jules who was stationed in Zimbabwe, formerly known as Rhodesia! It was a surprise to be invited. It gave me goosebumps. Why was this country going to be so special in my life that my visit was predicted so many years before?

I've spoken about my friendship with Jules throughout this book. We first met in 1998, at a cocktail party full of princes and princesses.

During the evening I made a comment that she still loves reminding me about: 'You're the only other normal person in this room besides me!' Of course, I was referencing the fact that the two of us were non-royals. Jules had just taken up a role working for one of the royal families and I was visiting for the first time as a guest of another royal family. Both of us were unfamiliar with socialising in noble circles. We clicked immediately.

Jules and I caught up again several days later at a hotel where she had found a wonderful little nook that was perfect for us to have a coffee and a chat. When it came time for her reading, I had to be careful as we were in a Muslim country. We looked as though we were just ladies of leisure chatting away. I held a piece of her jewellery in my hand, pretending I was admiring it, when really I was using it to hone in on her energies as I made predictions.

I don't *need* to hold anything to do a reading; I can look at someone and make forecasts. However, having something to hold is a signal for me that it's time to get to work. Without this little device I would never 'switch off'. I would be on high alert all the time, 'reading' whoever was around me. So I 'switch on' when I hold an item belonging to a person, or when I put my earphones on in the studio at the radio station. Apart from being in working mode, it allows my spirit guides to know that it's time to send the power to me, like electricity to a power point.

I will forget what I've said in a reading after it's finished. The information is simply given to me and I pass it on. It's as though I'm in a trance state that allows information to become obsolete once the reading is over. When I'm out of the altered state and a client wishes to discuss their reading or predictions, I'm able to recall *that* information. It's no different from having a normal conversation with a friend. I'm sure it's spirit's way of protecting the client's confidentiality and my safety. Anyway, Jules and I got along wonderfully and our paths crossed in a number of countries in the ensuing years. At these catch-up times, she would delight in declaring that she hadn't met the man she would supposedly marry. I'd seen that she'd meet him at a workshop where he would be standing at a lectern giving the lecture. Jules's professional life didn't blend with the workshop circuit, so she was sure it would never happen.

I have learned over the years that timing in the spirit world is fluid. That's because those in spirit do not understand how us earthly folk view time. Timing in their dimension is endless. They do not have a clock. It is as though, once leaving the earth plane, time goes in slow motion.

Working with spirit one must learn the art of patience and understand that divine timing isn't about deadlines. And often there's the joy of synchronicity at work as well. The great matchmaker in the sky needs all these aspects to align to make the magic happen. And, yes, we can alter fate, or seemingly misdirect it. It's like taking a detour when you're travelling to a destination because you missed the turn. Ultimately you get there, but more likely a little later than you had planned.

Never say never, though! A number of years later, circumstances indeed saw Jules attending a workshop, where she met the man at the lectern who gave the talk, and married him!

I first met Peter at their wedding in Ireland. He was exactly as I had predicted. They made a wonderful couple. My profession was rather difficult for him to embrace as he came from a very logical, disciplined, professional background. He was very open and frank about the fact that he didn't believe in psychics. I never have a problem with this as we are all entitled to our own belief systems. It certainly would be foolish to believe everything a psychic said—and I told him exactly that. We agreed to disagree. There's no need to try to convert someone, but I knew with every bone in my body that he would come around one day. I'm not a psychic for nothing!

Peter did confess that when he first met Jules—or, more accurately, bumped into her as she came out of the elevator—he had an overwhelming feeling of 'there goes my future'. I often find that men don't like the word 'premonition', but will often say in business that they have a gut feeling or a hunch that something will work. As the years have passed, Peter has become a firm believer with an open mind and heart around my predictions for him and Jules.

Spirit is grand—through Jules, Peter and their international circle of friends, I've received amazing invitations to visit exotic and distant shores where I've been able to further research the supernatural. Spirit had seen the connection that one day I would travel to Zimbabwe long before it happened. I responded to Jules's invitation immediately with, 'I'm coming! Count me in!'

My house is dotted with elephants of all different shapes, sizes and textures. Since I was a small child, I have always loved elephants. As I grew older I came to understand their significance associated with my spiritual path. As a symbol of wisdom, memory and intelligence, the elephant became my personal totem.

There was one obstacle to my African adventure: I was learning to walk again after major ankle surgery and three months confined to a wheelchair. My surgeon gave me the all-clear but I would still need to rely on a walking stick and firm shoes. It was suggested I consider purchasing Nordic walking poles to help with the uncertain terrain. I did follow the sensible advice; however, as I like life to be colourful, I purchased matching sticks in bright purples and pinks.

There's something magical about Zimbabwe; it is as though the earth speaks to you. The vibration from the ground, trees and people says, 'Hope'. The capital, Harare, where I stayed, had huge jacaranda trees lining both sides of the roads, forming a majestic flowering arch of blues and mauves. It was an umbrella that I was happy to walk under. Most locals walked to their destinations. Mornings were alive with a palette of colourful scenes—maids travelling to their workplaces were dressed in uniforms of pinks, greens, and crisp black and white. Laughing, eager, smartly dressed schoolchildren waited for their buses, and each corner seemed to have a pedlar selling phone cards. Everything was busy, busy, busy.

Winding down as the evening approached was a special time. Once Peter was home from work, the three of us sat out in the gardens, which had a lake and unusual local sculptures.

We'd sip gin and tonic, but the Bombay Sapphire was no ordinary gin: it contains a hand-selected array of botanicals—grains from West Africa, cubeb berries from Java, cassia bark from Indochina, almonds from Spain, and licorice from China! Coupled with the tonic, which contains quinine to assist in the prevention of malaria, I felt I was truly drinking a taste of history! Glass in hand, we relaxed and watched the colours of the African sunset dance, swirl and change their hues, all framed with a large Msasa tree—the type you see in movies where animals cluster for protection from the fierce African sun. A thousand green leaves were starting to sprout—a sign that the onset of the first rains would be approaching. It was so lovely—I felt privileged to be part of the land.

It was on one such evening that Peter recounted the story of 'The Elephant Walk'. It occurred in the year 2000 in Zimbabwe, in the midst of a wave of invasions and forced evictions of white-owned farms by government-sponsored gangs. A farmer had a herd of elephants near his land and he knew their fate would be sealed when the gangs took over, slaughtering them for their valuable ivory. The country was in a state of emergency and the elephants' fate weighed heavily on his heart. He had to do something, quickly.

The farmer knew a place about 50 kilometres away, where there was enough shelter, food and water and the elephants would be out of harm's way. It seemed a perfect solution. But, due to their huge size, number and wildness, it was impossible to move them in vehicles. The only option, he decided, was to walk with them.

But how do you muster and lead a herd of wild elephants to unfamiliar territory without it becoming your own suicide mission? Elephants are territorial and they like familiarity. They're vulnerable to emotion and they have phenomenal memories. From their perspective, their current home provided all their daily needs, including approximately 149–169 kilograms of vegetation and up to 212 litres of water! Why would they relocate to another place?

And, even if the farmer was successful in moving them, there was no guarantee that they wouldn't turn back and go home. But despite all these doubts and obstacles, the farmer knew what he had to do—for the sake of the elephants' lives, he had to try. He needed to dig deep into his soul and to harness all of his natural intuition and wisdom of spirit for the challenge ahead. The elephants' survival was now in his hands.

Remarkably, the wild elephants seemed to sense that they were in danger and understood the need to trust this human. The herd instinctively followed the farmer as he walked along dusty roads and through paddocks and dense scrub to the safety of their new home. Once they arrived, the farmer left them and hoped they would survive.

A number of years later, the political unrest had settled and the surrounding district was calmer and safer. The farmer often thought about those days marching the elephant herd to their new home and wondered whether they'd remained there and if they were still alive. To his surprise the elephants hadn't returned to their unsafe territory near his farm. Of course, they may have been killed trying to come back, or at their new location. He had to find out, so he decided to retrace his journey.

When he got to the location, he couldn't believe his eyes. There, before him, was the herd. Amazingly, they had stayed in the refuge and they were not only safe, they appeared to be very healthy.

A miracle had occurred because of an unspoken communication between a wild herd of elephants and one man, an interaction that gave a new generation of elephants the opportunity to survive and thrive.

Was it telepathic, or was it because of a supernatural experience that the elephants could read the man's thoughts or perhaps sense his fears for them that their territory was not safe anymore? Why did they follow him then stay in the new place? We will never know.

One thing is for sure, spirit is present in everything we do. It works for the benefit of all creation. As this story of the farmer shows, sometimes courage is required for you to step out of your comfort zone, take a chance, trust your intuition, and have faith that you will be guided by a higher power to pursue your good intentions.

18

SET IN STONE

My trip to Zimbabwe didn't come as a complete surprise. Spirit gave me warning during an energy/healing session that I had with qigong practitioner Grand Master Zhao. As I lay on his table, a figure from spirit emerged. This was not unusual. Often, when having treatments with Zhao I'd have spiritual experiences, visitations and messages.

Zhao's teacher–mentor, now in spirit, appeared and stood next to him. During my apprenticeship with spirit, along with my mother's teachings, I have learned to trust in the wisdom of spirit visitation, the visions and messages received. It is only with practice, trial and error that I have been able to accurately discern what I am seeing or hearing. For those of you embarking on your spiritual journey, baby steps are required before jumping in the deep end by acting upon what you perceive as a spiritual message or visitation. One must always be selective and cautious in this area. A fever, stress or some medications can bring an altered sense of reality that could pose a danger or be misleading.

After the spirit appeared, a large bird, like an eagle, flew over me, before another person in spirit appeared. The man was slender in build and dressed in white, with a long white beard. He positioned himself next to my head and told me, 'I am Moses.'

Was this the Moses of biblical times? At first I thought it couldn't be! And if it was, I really needed some confirmation, otherwise people might think I'd lost the plot!

Around his neck, he wore a necklace with a large blue stone. It was bright blue, the colour of lapis lazuli. He told me I was going to a place called Shona, and showed me a three-figure number starting with 7, informing me it would be the cost of my trip to Great Zimbabwe. He then spoke of my travels to come. I can't recall any more but was left wondering what was Shona and this eagle-like bird all about? And did Moses really wear a blue necklace?

As soon as I got home I started to research what this Moses had shown me. The trip to Zimbabwe was just a possibility at this stage. No bookings had been made. I was stunned to learn that the national bird of Zimbabwe was the very same bird I had seen in the visitation: the African fish eagle. More than this, there was a race of people called the Shona in Zimbabwe, and the bird had profound spiritual connections to these people as a symbol of protection and as a messenger of the gods that provided an ancestral link to heaven. I also discovered that there were famous soapstone carvings of the eagle on walls and monoliths of the ancient city of Great Zimbabwe. To top it off, I then learned that, apparently, the Ten Commandments handed to Moses were carved in sapphire, a stone worn on the garments of the priests!

Now I just had to go to Great Zimbabwe. I felt I'd been called there. When I finally received my travel quote, it was going to cost US$755—the three-figure number beginning with 7!

When I arrived in Zimbabwe I knew what I wanted—a Zimbabwe Bird statue, but I wanted it in a unique colour and texture. As a small child I had my own rock collection hidden in my wardrobe—much to the horror of my mother, who couldn't understand my affinity with rocks. I loved the feel of them as I held each one in my hands, the texture and their story, as if they were trying to tell me something of their heritage, their life. The Zimbabwean stone sculptures are hailed as one of Africa's original sources of artistic self-expression on the international art scene. The name Zimbabwe itself is a celebration of the country's early stone buildings and sculpture. These unique stone sculptures also celebrate Shona spirituality and their link to the Bird God and heaven. Zimbabwe adopted the bird as the country's emblem and symbol of freedom, which is proudly displayed on their national flag and coat of arms as well as currency and stamps.

Jules has some truly amazing large pieces. I longed to pack them up and take them home! But one small piece would be perfect for me, and Jules was happy to help me find it.

It was hot, dry and dusty as we stepped out of the jeep to inspect the huge display of stone statues on the roadside. We were followed by the local stallholders, who begged and pleaded with us to buy their wares. You couldn't blame them. Tourism had come to a standstill, the local currency was worthless and people were out of work; the meagre profits they made would enable them to survive another day.

There was an array of every kind of statue as I walked up and down the row of stalls looking for the statue that would call me. Suddenly I felt a zapping, a draining of my energy source. I knew I was under psychic attack.

Jules commented, 'You've just lost all the colour in your face, like you do at Scott's Market!'

She was referring to our times in Rangoon, Burma. Every time I went to the markets there, within minutes of walking in, I always had the same reaction. Scott's Market, now called Bogyoke Market, was well-known for its antiques, gems, semiprecious stones and an assortment of 'black market' activities. The energies there were dense, of a lower frequency. Many stallholders and their wares—as well as the local customers—would have been subjected to political pressure, torture or even slavery. Their residual energy bank held great darkness and sadness. The negative energies they carried around had the potential to jump ship onto a higher frequency individual.

I started to feel faint and needed to leave. I knew within my being that the beautiful items before me held a history of violence, bloodshed and deep sadness. The people selling the stone statues, the artists who made the products or their families would have been part of those experiences, or the stones themselves held the memories of the past. Before me was a dark energy of souls reaching out, seeking freedom from bondage, pain and oppression, like a drowning person seeks a life raft.

As I turned to walk back to the jeep, I spotted the bird statue I'd wished for. It was majestic, beautiful, in a very unusual shade of green with little veins of white and yellow running through it. Jules took over the financial transactions as I made my way to the jeep. I have learned so much from her over the years about bargaining. She will always, always, get the best price.

When we arrived home, I lovingly bathed my bird statue in water to cleanse away the energy of the past. I was doubly careful and cleaned it with a sage-stick smudging as well.

There was no way I could return to those street stalls again. So the next day we went to an art gallery that had grounds where the local stone artists were making their sculptures. It was indeed a very different energy. These people loved what they were doing. They worked outside in a contented, fulfilled way. Although they were paid on commission for their products, there was no middle man, so the energies were purer. The artists were relaxed and very happy to talk about their projects, and allow photos to be taken.

I bought some wonderful pieces. There's a unique beauty within each stone, waiting for the master craftsman to come along and re-fashion the raw product. So, too, the people of this country will be re-fashioned over time and their sense of pride and hope will once again return to the lands formerly called the 'bread basket' of Africa. My Zimbabwe statues will be a constant reminder of the plight of these people.

Once more, there were important insights from this experience. Residual energy is contained in all matter—memories of the past are like DNA of the soul, holding a bank of information, much like crumbs of a cake, bits and pieces there for the collecting if you care to. Most people wouldn't be bothered with stale crumbs. Such is the case with residual energy—you either choose to allow the DNA crumbs that are held within the object to come home with you, or you leave them well enough alone.

Many people don't understand when they enter a place or hold an object why they get a sense that it 'feels right' or there's something 'not right' about it. We are naturally and intuitively tuning into our senses, at times not heeding the information we are sensing. As an extreme sensitive, these negative energies can knock me for six, literally zapping my energy source. So care must always be taken when acquiring objects, new or used—even clothes you buy should be washed or purified with burning sage or smudging to release stored residual energy.

19

REAL LIFE MAGIC

I was on my way to one of the most spectacular sights on the planet when I had devastating news: 'All flights to Victoria Falls have been cancelled—all domestic airline crew have been sacked,' Jules told me.

We sat down for coffee to explore the options. With a six- to nine-hour nonstop drive through Zimbabwe before us, terrible road conditions and road rules nonexistent, we figured we'd have to cancel the safari or hope that the airlines resumed. No-one fancied the long-haul drive, so we decided to sleep on it.

The next morning I bounded down to breakfast and announced that the planes would be back in the air on Wednesday, which meant we would be able to fly to the falls. My friends were stunned and rather perplexed as they enquired where I heard the news—Was it on the television or the radio? Well, neither, actually—it was a direct broadcast from the spirit world. I had asked my guides prior to going to bed to let me know when the planes would return and their answer was as clear as an airport announcement: 'Planes will be in the air on Wednesday.'

The expressions on Jules and Peter's faces said it all: You must be kidding! True, all the crews had been sacked by the government, bringing internal flights to a standstill. But later that day we learned they had outsourced, using flight staff from South Africa, and minimal services would start on Wednesday—so we were off. Never doubt the word of spirit!

I can't tell you the joy I felt knowing that I was finally going to see wild elephants in their natural setting. I was like a child waiting for her birthday party.

It was a short internal flight and an hour's drive to our Victoria Falls accommodation. The vegetation reminded me so much of the Australian bush—dry, red and scattered. The locals walked or, as the driver explained, the more wealthy had a donkey to cart their belongings. Young children watched patiently over herds of goats as if they had all the time in the world. I was excited when I saw my first group of warthogs race across the road.

A dinner cruise had been booked for early evening along the Zambezi River so there wasn't much time to pause. A quick shower and change and we were off again. As the bus wound its way towards the river front, I couldn't help but notice the large mounds of excrement scattered everywhere—on the road and throughout the bush.

The bus driver explained they were telltale signs that elephants had visited; in fact, the elephants were in plague proportions in the local town. Coming to the end of the dry season, they were desperate for fresh pickings of vegetation and the well-maintained resorts provided a wonderful bounty for them. Not surprisingly, the elephants targeted the resorts, especially during the night, and a number of hotels had been raided and many of their beautiful trees and gardens totally destroyed. The herd numbers were huge and the elephants unstoppable.

I could hear the beating of African drums as we pulled closer to the boat moorings. Locals dressed in full tribal costume lined the shore. Their drum music gave me goosebumps, not of fear, but excitement—I was really here, in Africa!

Our boat had all the old-world charm of highly polished wood. A guide talked up the history of the two countries of Zambia and Zimbabwe which bordered the river to Victoria Falls. Yes, there were wild animals, but the unpredictable waters could be just as dangerous. Only the day before a little motorboat with two Australians on board had gone over one of the smaller rapids and capsized. The two tourists survived, but their local guide never surfaced.

We glided past monkeys and crocodiles on the foreshore. A water snake wiggled past. Then I saw him—a bull elephant on a small island. He was huge; bigger than I had ever imagined. He had obviously waded over to pick at some inviting vegetation. Bulls lead a solitary life, only seeking the company of females when it's time for mating. I wondered if he was lonely. He looked almost marooned. The boat went closer and closer, and I was able to get some wonderful photos.

Then someone yelled out, 'Hippos!'. There were several mums with their little ones. You needed to be patient, waiting for them to resurface to get a glimpse or two. When they did, the babies looked so cute, all pink and grey and cuddly. Oh, how I would have loved to give them a big hug! But we were told their looks are deceiving as hippos are responsible for more deaths in Africa than is any other native animal.

That night I slept well. Perhaps it was the combination of the fresh, dry African air, fatigue and a childhood dream partly becoming a reality. I was satisfied.

Breakfast had to be early, as I was to embark on the second part of my childhood fantasy, riding an elephant. Because of my ankle-fusion operation, my mobility was limited. The tour guide had arranged a solo half-day trip to an elephant park, rather than being in a convoy of riders.

My heart was racing as I stepped out of the vehicle, walking stick in one hand and camera in the other. A hot breakfast and a pot of tea were waiting for me as they informed me about the dos and don'ts of riding an elephant.

Then I spotted the elephants with riders on their backs walking towards me. They had brought two for my selection. One was a very tall, mature elephant and the other was slightly smaller. I heard quite clearly from spirit: 'Choose the smaller one.' Interestingly, his name was Houdini. Were my spirit guides having fun with this magical name from the past? I don't know, but I'm glad I listened, as I would never have managed to mount the larger of the two.

Houdini was positioned next to a platform and I had to walk up a small flight of stairs to climb onto his back. Houdini's 'saddle' was merely a padded throw-over affair, with stirrups and a handle to hold; not like the chairs you see on elephants in Thailand. As much as I tried I couldn't throw my leg over his large back.

We all started to laugh—it looked as though I was never going to be able to get on. But the elephant handlers had an idea. They would get several men to lift me—yes, lift me! I am no small mamma to lift, but lift me they did, and plonked me onto the back of Houdini. Hours later, when I viewed the video of the excursion, I laughed and laughed. It would have been perfect for *Funniest Home Videos* or a comedy sketch.

I have to admit I felt scared. The small handle I had to hold onto seemed insecure, so I asked the guide if I could put my arms around his waist. Walking by our side was a guard with a rifle. We were in the national park where wild elephants roam. Elephants have an acute sense of smell; the idea was that the wild elephants would smell gun powder, recognise that it was dangerous and hopefully stay away.

It wasn't the most comfortable ride; my legs were straddled over Houdini's very broad back as we loped along. A flash of the movie *Blazing Saddles* went through my mind: the men alighting from their horses, legs wide apart, stiff and uncomfortable! I was glad I wore jeans and a long-sleeve shirt, as Houdini would stop and have a feed at whatever took his fancy and at time the prickles from the various bushes would brush against my body.

Suddenly, my guide seemed agitated. He pushed Houdini to a canter, explaining later there was a swarm of bees nearby and elephants do not like bees. I came to realise that this was not just a fun experience but a real-life experience. A herd of impalas darted in front of us. To the left was a group of warthogs. And in the distance the sound of an elephant trumpeting seemed to vibrate through the trees and right through my body.

'Are you all right, ma'am?' enquired my guide. 'You seem tense.'

Too right I was tense! We now were deep into the Zimbabwean bush. My head was spinning as the heat of the day pounded down on me, and coupled with the fear factor of what I had got myself into, I decided it was time to return to base.

It was then that I finally relaxed, and was able to appreciate the experience Houdini was giving me. We passed a small lagoon that was home to several crocodiles and I appreciated the security of riding high on my elephant's back. Feeling more secure, I was able to take in the information that my guide was telling me about the African bush and elephants. And wasn't that what I had come for, after all?

As we neared the end of our ride, the thought that started rushing through my mind was how on earth I was going to get off this animal! It turned out to be far easier than getting on. The men were there to assist me again. We all cheered as I placed my feet on the ground. It felt good to be earthbound again. I limped away, not only with a stiff ankle but now also with a sore bum—what a sight I was! Yet I had a feeling of accomplishment. But better was to come.

After a refreshing drink, the handlers brought Houdini and the larger elephant to me to pat. It was then I made the connection. Houdini' eyes and mine met and an exchange of energies pulsated through my body. I felt a deep reassurance that he would never put me in danger. He was a friend. I lovingly stroked his hard, dry, wrinkled skin. The stiff, tough hairs protruding from his hide prickled my fingers. It wasn't the most pleasant sensation, but I was thrilled at the same time. I had been given a bag of treats to feed both elephants and I have to say that was the most enjoyable part of the experience—the one-on-one time I had with Houdini. The elephants were my totems—they were my soul connections.

It is important for the survival of the planet that we respect all creatures. They give us so much without asking for anything in return. If we could take a leaf out of their book of life, what a wonderful place this planet would be.

20

SPIRITS IN KIND

I had many magical elephant moments in Zimbabwe which I will treasure all my life. But there was one which stood out, as it proved to me that all living things are capable of feeling, and our souls are all connected by spirit.

The four of us—Jules, Peter, their daughter and myself—along with several other tourists from various countries, piled into a small van headed for Zimbabwe's largest national park, Hwange. The trip was dusty, dry and cramped. Some of the others slept, but I couldn't see the point. Why come so far without taking in what was offered—scenery, skyline, people and atmosphere?

We passed through little villages where mud huts, chickens, goats and plenty of children dotted the landscape. We drove over numerous bridges where there was very little running water below us. It was coming to the end of the dry season and everyone was looking forward to the heavy rains to refresh the land and their hopes.

The reality was stark—we have so much and they have so little. I felt warm inside that my slight contribution through tithing went to support a number of children and their communities, providing fresh water, and health and education programs.

Then, as if to remind us of our purpose, we saw movement in the trees. It was tall, orange, black and cream—our first sighting of a group of giraffes! It was real! We were in Africa and on our way to a safari!

Very soon we were at the big iron gates that led into the national park. The guards obligingly opened the gates, and our vehicle made its way to the refreshment bay where several different four-wheel drives waited patiently for the new intake of visitors.

Our bags were now in the trailer marked 'The Hide'. We were ready to jump in and travel further, deep into the park for our safari experience. I got to ride in the front with the driver. What a blessing that turned out to be—I had more comfort and padding and some degree of protection from the hot wind and dust that my friends and fellow guests were enduring. It was a bumpy ride as we navigated the subtropical thorn and sand flats on the edge of the Kalahari Desert.

The park has a colourful past. It was once home to the nomadic San bushmen, who lived and feasted off the great herds of migrating game. In time they were displaced by stronger African tribes, who in turn were overtaken by the arrival of white men.

We passed zebras, impalas, herds of giraffes and unusual birds—but not elephants! I was told I had to wait until the cooler hours of the day, as elephants tended to hide under the foliage to protect themselves from the intense heat. Closer to nightfall they would come out for water and I was guaranteed a sighting—after all, the park boasted 30 000 of them, so I was confident I would be granted my wish.

The accommodation was tent-style but very comfortable. Each tent was like a cabin with canvas sides and a hard floor and all the mod cons: a shower, toilet and verandah with chairs that looked over the local waterhole.

We were given strict instructions that once we were in our tents at night-time, we were not to leave them at all until daylight. The previous night, a small deer had been sighted enjoying the warmth of the woodchip water heater that supplied each tent with its hot water, only to be attacked and killed by a leopard!

I didn't sleep well that night. Baboons were jumping from tent to tent. There were calls of wild dogs in the distance. I could hear branches crunching as something walked around my tent. I learned in the morning from one of the guards that it was deer who came in for the small green pickings that grew near the local water outlets.

Then, as morning broke I heard, 'Georgina, come quickly—quickly, outside!' It was the excited voice of Jules who was standing outside my tent facing the direction of the waterhole.

A procession of elephants was making its way to the waterhole. Seemingly in slow motion, they came from all directions—there were elephants, elephants and more elephants. Soon the waterhole was surrounded. Some gently drank from the water's edge. Others rolled in the muddy banks. The newest additions stayed close to their mothers. At times you could hear the roar of a bull elephant in the distance, trumpeting to all that he was on his way. Baboons, zebras and buffalo joined with the elephants, all drinking from the precious life source. I was in elephant paradise.

The guides told us how several days earlier they had pulled the carcass of an elephant from one of the waterholes. They had watched the animal's slow demise the previous week as it lingered around the site, but they knew nature must take its course. Unfortunately, it had died in the water, which would become polluted if the body was left to decay. So the remains had to be pulled from the water and relocated a little distance away—but not too far.

We humans don't have a monopoly on grief. Like us, elephants are capable of complex emotions. When they suffer the loss of a loved one, they also grieve. They have even been known to express their sadness over a stillborn calf. The expressions on the mother's face, her sad eyes and drooping ears are all telltale signs of an elephant grieving. They have been seen covering a deceased elephant with leaves, twigs and branches. And if a herd encounters an elephant's skeleton on their travels, each might pick up a bone and hide it under a bush.

Because deceased loved ones are so important to elephants, it was crucial that the remains of this particular elephant be left close by the common drinking grounds, so its family would be able to carry out their grieving. After the removal of the body from the waterhole, the guides had seen a number of elephants standing over it and touching it with their trunks as though they were in mourning.

There were no other elephants present when we viewed the carcass, only a tree full of vultures dropping, diving and devouring the remains that lay on the parched, dry earth. It was sad. We were told that the bones would be left in the same place for the returning elephants to grieve over. They would not only touch the flesh, but would also stroke and touch the skeletal remains with their trunks.

The elephants' mourning process reminded me of how I tune into a reading by holding an object that someone has worn, where there exists a residual memory bank, a powerhouse of energy and information. I wondered, were the elephants capable of tapping into this energy and connecting with their beloved? I thought about my sessions with my clients who seek comfort in Dearly Departed readings, wanting to talk with their deceased loved ones and wishing they could still touch them. Was this also the theme for elephants? Perhaps this was why I had always felt an affinity for these animals.

Our days on safari were full and flew by—early morning trips before breakfast scouting for game, more excursions after breakfast, then a siesta after lunch to avoid the hottest part of the day, perfectly timed in harmony with most animals finding refuge in the dense scrub from the harsh midday sun, and a late afternoon tour in the hope of spotting more of the wildlife as they ventured out for water and sustenance.

On our last day, I opted to stay and observe the elephants at the waterhole, rather than take an excursion to a remote part of the park. As I sat watching them, I wondered for how many centuries had herds of elephants called these sacred lands home. How many times had they drunk from this waterhole? How many had given birth to the next generation here? And how many had passed to the other side?

As the sunset hid behind the trees and the almost-full moon danced in the sky, hues of purple, pink and orange presented a kaleidoscope of shapes and patterns. As if on cue, the parade started.

The elephants began to leave the waterhole, almost in a straight line and always led by the very large matriarch. The calves held onto the tails of their mothers with their cute little rubbery trunks, followed by older siblings and aunties. They rambled along, heading back into the African scrub.

I had much to be grateful for. The elephants had taught me many things. We are not that dissimilar in family structures. We grieve the same. It was obvious why I had intuitively chosen elephants to be my totem all those years ago. We share a deep spiritual alliance, a bond, a kinship that comes from ancient wisdom.

21

MY SPIRIT COMPANION

It was rather a rushed goodbye as Jules and Peter dropped me off at the majestic Victoria Falls Hotel, affectionately referred to as the Grand Old Lady of the Falls. They had just enough time to catch their flight back to Harare. I would be joining them several days later. I still had more dreams to fulfil.

The hotel was familiar to me, as we'd stayed there several days before our departure to Hwange National Park. My room had been very comfortable but nothing compared to the very posh stateroom I was ushered into. Rushing through my mind was 'How much extra is this going to cost me?' I rang the front desk to discover that my generous friends had upgraded me.

I was just in time for the afternoon high tea served on the terrace that overlooked the falls. What a spectacular view! You could hear the noise of the waters pounding and roaring as they flowed over the rocky plateaus. It was easy to see why the falls form the largest sheet of cascading water in the world.

The first European to see the falls, the Scottish missionary and explorer David Livingstone, named them in honour of Queen Victoria. The indigenous name is Mosi-oa-Tunya, which means smoke that thunders. And that's what the mist looks and sounds like—smoke bellowing as it rises into the air.

One of the attractions of the hotel was also one of its biggest problems—large, cheeky and mischievous baboons. The staff would try to frighten them off with brooms and sticks, but they would simply scurry up the trees as if to say, 'You can't catch me!' From the trees the baboons inspected each hotel window to see if it was open. Then they would manoeuvre their bodies through any gaps into the hotel suites. As quickly as they entered, they left with a piece of fruit, a bag or whatever caught their eye.

I just had enough time to walk through the gardens of the hotel, escorted by a guard to the Victoria Falls entry. It was a struggle as the ground was sandy and at times rocky. On arrival at the gate, a guide suggested I use a wheelchair to sightsee. How that man pushed me around to show me as much as he did in such a short amount of time is a miracle.

It was full moon, a unique time for viewing the falls, because the reflection of the moon on the water presents a 'moonbow', which can be seen in the spray instead of the usual daylight rainbow. I felt so fortunate to witness the moonbow. It was magnetic and inspiring.

Being so close and feeling the power of the falls—their energy, their life—was breathtaking. It was so different from my previous stay, when I took a helicopter flight that followed the flow of the river down into the falls and below. This time I was standing right next to the water and felt its cool and refreshing spray on my face. I felt that there was something far greater at work—its purpose! With the busyness of the world—fast-paced technology, people wanting instant results—the magnetism of the falls exerts its own special force of attraction. For a moment, minutes or even hours, the falls give us the opportunity to be healed by their essence and strength. It is a powerful gift from nature. I was in awe.

Returning to the hotel I was overcome with exhaustion. It had been a big day, travelling hours by jeep through Hwange National Park, then the tour of the falls. There was just enough time for me to have a shower and then quickly walk through the expansive grounds to the smorgasbord dinner under the stars. The Zimbabwean stone statues dotted through the gardens seemed as if they had doubles as the moonlight danced and toyed with their reflections in the water.

Suddenly, I was missing the companionship of my friends, as everyone else was seated in tour groups or with friends or partners, while I had been placed at a table by myself. The entertainment was provided by the local villagers—a spectacular display of tribal dance and song—and I tried to get into the swing of it, taking photo after photo to occupy my time, but it wasn't enough. I kept thinking, I just wish I wasn't by myself tonight. I took another photo, then another.

As I ate my dessert, I decided to look through the photos I'd taken. There, sandwiched between two other photos, was a face—not of a human, but a spirit! I hurriedly zoomed in to magnify the features

I was observing. The figure looked warrior-like, with a large head and a thin, small body. I wasn't alone after all!

Captured on the camera was the spirit I believed had been with me the entire trip, looking after me and keeping me safe. I couldn't work out if the warrior was male or female, so I chose to give it the name 'Spirit of Africa'.

When I arrived back in Sydney I uploaded the photos to my computer so I could examine my findings, but there was only one picture in which the spirit appeared. Even the most sceptical of friends had to agree that this one showed the spirit. It was large, it was clear, it was real. Did the full moon's unusual energies attract the spirit? Or was it the tribal dancing and singing that brought about its presence? Or perhaps it was my wish to have company? No matter what the answer was or is, that night at Victoria Falls Hotel, the spirit realm heard my prayer and I did not dine alone!

22

ANCIENT CITY, ANCIENT SECRETS

I was mesmerised as I watched a television program focusing on megaliths around the world that were built on earth grid points. These grid points are areas that maximise the earth's energy which flows through and around the planet interacting with our energy fields, not dissimilar to how acupuncture operates on points in our body. When these grids intersect, a powerful energy vortex occurs. One in particular made my heart jump—it was a city surrounded by a great wall. There was a stirring in my soul, a sense of familiarity. Had I been there before? It was somewhere in Africa, but I'd no idea where—I just knew I had to go there.

Many years later I came across pictures of the city as I did research for my trip to Africa. It was Great Zimbabwe, which spirit had told me I would visit. Was it luck or part of the divine plan for my soul?

ANCIENT CITY, ANCIENT SECRETS

As the car that was to take me there pulled up to Jules's house, we were surprised to see it wasn't the most modern of motor vehicles for a four-hour drive. There were more surprises to come. The safety belts at the back didn't work, nor did the air conditioner, but my guide was friendly, extremely knowledgeable and a great driver.

I became excited as I sighted large boulders and rock formations, familiar from the photos of the ruins I had seen. I knew we must be very near our destination, Great Zimbabwe, which had been the largest medieval city in sub-Saharan Africa, with a population of up to 18 000 people. There were rumours that pyramids were first built on this site. The royal palace was positioned on the highest point, protected by amazing feature walls, more than 5 metres high and constructed without mortar. I just hoped I would have the energy and strength to climb the many steps.

We pulled into an African-type resort, with a swimming pool, main reception centre and little huts dotted throughout the grounds. The first challenge came at dinner time. The generator was unpredictable and the lights around the resort would come and go. I was handed a large lantern to find my way around my room, and for use outside when I made my way to the dining room for meals. I could hear the baboons, which I'd been told were aggressive, calling nearby.

The sunset was spectacular—oranges, pinks, golds and purples—what a way to end the day! Better still, the next day would be spent at the ruins.

Nothing could have prepared me for the extent of Great Zimbabwe. My guide said these were the largest ruins in Africa the remains of an important commercial centre and powerful political kingdom. In the medieval period it had been one of the most significant trading regions for gold, iron, copper, tin, cattle and cowry shells. During excavations, many items from other lands were found—glassware from Syria, a minted coin from Kilwa in Tanzania, and Persian and Chinese ceramics from the thirteenth and fourteenth centuries.

My heart leapt when the guide spoke about the most important artefacts to be recovered from the site—the eight Zimbabwe Birds from on top of the monoliths. The carved soapstone birds were the height of people. I marvelled at the similarity between the soapstone birds in the museum and the one I had purchased in Harare—the colour and shape were so similar.

We set off on foot to the Hill Complex, the Valley Complex and the Great Enclosure. The Hill Complex was believed to be the original site of the Zimbabwe Birds, which had stood on the highest point that overlooked the entire Eastern Enclosure. To me the birds were like totems, gods selected to watch over the royal family and their people. They were their protectors, watchdogs and guides—spirit forms warding off anything of evil intent. My guide liked my interpretation and said it sat well with him. As I gazed about me, the vision I had during the qigong healing session in Zhao's rooms of the large bird that flew over me started flooding back. What did it mean? Was I being told I would be protected by spirit on my visit to this land? Or was the spirit of the Bird God calling me?

We moved on to the Great Enclosure, inner and outer walls encircling a series of structures. Walking in between the walls was an eerie feeling. There were no other tourists, just the guide and myself. At times our voices echoed as if we were in unison with something greater. Why was the enclosure built? The royal household had lived on the highest point, where they could be safe. I felt like I was in a fort with such high walls that no-one could have penetrated without being seen. It felt strange that such a huge structure seemed stranded in the middle of nowhere. But then my guide reminded me of the wealth of the land, the gold and minerals traded with other tribes and nations, and the need for security from warring tribes and invaders.

We continued walking in what seemed to be a huge circle which became smaller and smaller as we reached the middle point. An energy was emerging. Had our walking created a spiral or vortex, much like a spinning top going around and around? We had come full circle.

When I enquired whether the inhabitants of this great city were Jewish, my guide confirmed they were an ethnic group with traditions of ancient Jewish or South Arabian descent passed through their male line. This struck a chord; though I am not Jewish, I've found myself drawn to Judaism for years. It feels very familiar to me—like a distant memory of other times.

They say these forebears came in ships to obtain gold. They were known for their exceptional skills as miners and metal workers. They were the originators and masters of the art of circumcision: within the grounds, significant models of circumcised male organs had been found. Some say they were one of the lost tribes of Israel. Those who claim to be descendants still, to this day, practise many of the Jewish rituals and traditions, and claim to be of that faith.

The vortex of energy I had sensed penetrating into my feet from the ground was becoming stronger. I had a recollection of a discussion

I'd had with my friend Elaine in America around the theory that the earth has a matrix grid and energy system that nourishes our planet, flowing through the centre of the Earth from the Laptev Sea to Antarctica. Elaine explained that these vortexes were masses of energy that move in a rotary or whirling motion creating depressions or vacuums at their centre. They are just like the energy system in our bodies with their personal vortexes called chakras (the Sanskrit word for wheel). All of these vortexes transmit and receive energy information to the matrix.

There exists unison between the way the planet works and the human body. When we're in sacred places, it's much easier to align beautifully through these powerful energy fields available to us. My guide didn't quite get what I was talking about, but interestingly he had been told there was a geographical line from Zimbabwe up to somewhere in Israel or Egypt, and that his country was considered the foundation of this energy line.

It helped to explain the feeling I was getting up my spine: a tingling sensation—like the charge of static electricity when you touch a door handle on a windy day—followed by a lovely warm rush of energy. Perhaps, just perhaps, the ancients were drawn to the magnetic energy of this land. Was that why monoliths of such greatness had been built here and also in Egypt? Were they guided by a higher power to create such an extraordinary place? Were the ancient tribes wise enough to pick Great Zimbabwe not just for its wealth of resources but for something far more important? Were they aware of how powerful the energy force was here—that same energy that was the base of all creation?

ANCIENT CITY, ANCIENT SECRETS

As I walked alone between the two walls and contemplated these thoughts, I was attuning my body to the pulse of Mother Earth. I felt the vibration of the Kundalini—the great life force of this land—rising through my feet, up into my spine, all the way to my head. Was this what the ancient ones had felt, a life force like no other that propelled them to greatness? Did these past civilisations combine their knowledge of the constellations and Mother Earth to work in harmony with each other? It literally was a marriage made of heaven and earth. I needed to ask Mother Earth what she wanted me to know about these places I had for many years longed to visit. Was there something more significant, a deeper lesson for me and others to learn?

I kept hearing the word 'balance'. Then it dawned on me how simple it was. It was the life force under my feet and above my head. I was being shown the secrets our forebears had learned—being in balance with nature. As humans, we have lost our alignment, become off-balance and are now out of sync with the energies of this planet. There is an urgency, a calling out to bring our lives and that of the Earth's back into the rhythm that once existed so we can live and sustain the planet in harmony and balance.

As we drove away from Great Zimbabwe I felt privileged that I had been chosen to visit these ancient lands and learn their secrets. They were affirming that it is not too late for us to rescue the planet.

23

FALLEN SOLDIERS

Through friendships, we can find ourselves in all kinds of unexpected situations. When I predicted Jules, my client and later my friend, would meet her husband-to-be, Peter, at a lecture, I'd no idea they'd set their wedding for the Irish spring. The date was far closer than I'd anticipated and I just couldn't see how my finances at the time would allow me to get there with such short notice.

With only two weeks left before the big day, Jules touched down in Dublin to finalise all the arrangements. How I wished I was there! Over the years since our first meeting we had managed to catch up in a number of countries and emailed regularly, yet I still hadn't met the man who had captured her heart.

Then I received an unexpected phone call from an editor of a magazine. The conversation came around to my schedule and then my prediction about Jules's wedding and her invitation. There was a pause, and then an offer was put to me: 'If you can come up with four unique stories around Ireland, I'll consider assisting you with a cash advance.'

I only had half an hour to submit the draft proposal. I'm sure spirit took over. Concepts of fairies, leprechauns, matchmaking festivals and Celtic wisdom sprang immediately to mind. And, you guessed it, the magazine editor agreed to my ideas.

'I'm coming, I'm coming to your wedding!' I screamed to Jules down the phone.

We didn't know if I'd get a flight at such short notice, or even hotel accommodation, but I knew already that luck was with me, or perhaps it was Celtic magic at work!

Equally spooky was the fact that my friend Jennifer was off to another friend's wedding in London. I remember her friend coming for a reading. She was so distressed with my predictions I had to make her a cup of tea to calm her down. My job is not to have people in tears, but when spirit has guidance I must tell what I'm shown faithfully and accurately, to help the person before me.

Her boyfriend at the time loved tennis, and she had her heart set on marrying him. But in her reading I spoke of a man who was a professional tennis player, and wore a uniform with shining buttons. It was not the man she was with. Devastated that I wouldn't give her boyfriend the nod of approval, the client burst into tears. Eventually the relationship ended. She left Australia broken-hearted to try her luck in London, where she fell in love with a plain-clothes detective.

Once, when she was visiting his home, he opened his wardrobe and showed her his police uniform, with the shining buttons. But her biggest surprise was to come when she told him about my predictions. She laughed at the suggestion he was a professional tennis player. Shocked by this revelation, as he didn't believe in psychics, he admitted that prior to entering the police force he had been a professional tennis player!

Jennifer's plan was to attend her friend's wedding and then travel to Ireland in search of her family roots. Coincidentally we'd be there at the same time. So an idea was hatched. After Jules's wedding, we would hire a car and explore the Emerald Isle together.

It was a 30-hour plane trip so I spent my first night in accommodation near the airport, where I had a good night's sleep, then transferred to another hotel within walking distance of the wedding venue. The small family-run hotel in downtown Dublin was surrounded by beautiful Georgian architecture, but it had no elevator, which meant my oversized bag had to be dragged up three flights of stairs. I caught up with Jules, and finally met Peter—who was, of course, wonderful—over a high tea, but still suffering from jet lag, I decided I needed another early night.

Soon after going to bed, I woke to the sounds of clanging, digging and men talking. Some were shouting. The language sounded foreign to me. I got cold shivers as I heard screams. It sounded like a war zone outside! The noise continued into the early hours of the morning. I wasn't impressed. Why were people allowed to work on a construction site at night so close to a hotel?

Half-dead with tiredness I dragged myself down to breakfast the next morning. The Australian receptionist was keen to talk. 'How did you sleep?' she asked.

When I told her about the noise, the colour drained from her face. Then, when she explained why she was shocked, it was my turn to be surprised.

The receptionist said there hadn't been any work going on at that site for quite some time, let alone at night. Work had stopped there because they uncovered a Viking burial ground and found the remains of four young men, along with knives, shield bosses, combs and some decorated pins. A newspaper report stated their remains were situated around the edge of the original *Dubh Linn*, or 'black pool', from which Dublin got its name, and the burial ground probably dates to around 670–882 AD.

Then she waved a brochure in front of me about the Dublin ghost-busting tour. 'You might experience more of the same,' she said excitedly.

My initial reaction was, as if I wanted another spirit encounter! Then I thought, why not? I've been to haunted churches, graveyards and all manner of spooky sights.

So I went along on the ghost tour and was surprised when people screamed as they 'felt' paranormal experiences. Was it just a set-up? Perhaps the ghosts were sleeping, because I didn't feel a thing!

I couldn't get the previous night's experience out of my mind, so I decided to do some of my own research on South Great Georges Street, Dublin. I discovered the majority of these burial sites dated back to the ninth century AD, a period when Dublin was home to a large Viking longphort—a defended base used to raid the surrounding countryside. Here, their fleets were moored and large numbers of warriors passed through its gates in search of wealth and riches through force of arms. They also established one of Europe's largest slave markets. Archaeological evidence suggests that for many Vikings their only reward was a shallow grave. As pagan warriors, these casualties of the Irish campaigns were typically buried with militaristic items, such as swords, spears, shields and daggers, for use in the afterlife. Were these ancient Viking spirits trying to reach out to me? I suspect this was more a case of residual energy. The recordings and energies of that distant time when the Vikings held sway had imprinted in the earth, rocks and metal implements. The excavation of the land along with the Vikings' implements had released the energy that had been stored there. It was like a playback of events that had occurred and were still available to be accessed by a sensitive who is able to tune in.

This process is similar to when you record a television show and then replay it later. Just as video and audio tapes capture sound and images on a film, material that has been oxidised or rusted (like iron), certain building materials (such as slate used in older castles), and stone structures can all store energy. When a traumatic event or a time of heightened emotions occurs, these materials record the event for future playback. While this may take a bit to get your head around, don't forget that everything is made up of energy, and energy cannot be destroyed.

That night when I was kept awake by the noise and activity outside my hotel room, I must have experienced a playback of scenes, sounds and events from the Viking past. This got me thinking—would my psychic ability allow me to tap into or experience playbacks from other cultures, civilisations and countries? I was hooked!

24

WHEN SPIRIT COMES CALLING

Spirit reaches out in all kinds of ways—and times—including the most inhospitable times. It was 4 a.m. Not another dream! It was cold and I didn't have the inclination to get up and type out what I had just experienced. But past lessons have taught me to obey when spirit beckons, otherwise I would have to learn another lesson to remind me.

The dream was for my client Josie. She'd initially had a postal reading, having just moved to Munich in Germany after a marriage breakdown. She had a new job in the motor industry and was keen to learn what lay ahead.

She wasn't too impressed with my warning of an imminent pregnancy, which she'd avoided in her marriage. But spirit had the final say when it was later confirmed that she was, indeed, pregnant after a whirlwind romance. They married, bought a house and lived a happy-ever-after lifestyle in affluent Bavaria.

Eventually, as fate would have it, Josie and I finally came face-to-face when I travelled overseas for my friends Jules and Pete's wedding. We had lunch and she filled me in on how her reading had played out. Her life was perfect, and so Josie didn't imagine that she'd be receiving any more predictions from spirit in the near future.

But then I had my dream. I knew it was for Josie, though I wasn't sure how to tell her about it, as the dream was quite obscure and we hadn't been in contact for several years. Still, I knew it had been given to me for a good reason—spirit doesn't waste time on trivialities! I quickly typed an email explaining why I was contacting her after so long. I knew she would understand, as her Indian cultural heritage led her to believe in premonitions, dreams and signs.

In the dream I was in a huge multistorey office block, with windows on every side. From one side the view was all sand and on the other there was an ocean, with a wharf and ships docked. There was a knock at the door, which I opened to let Josie in. I was wrapping Christmas presents to hide from the children. I beckoned her to come and look outside the windows and take in the views from all sides. I then turned to Josie and told her that she would make the right choice. It would be right for her in every way. It would be successful. (There was one part of the dream I didn't tell her because I thought it was about the past—oh, how wrong I was!) I sent the email, turned off my computer and went back to bed.

When I switched on the computer in the morning, there was an urgent email reply from Josie, saying she needed to be in touch. She was just about to attend a scheduled meeting with her boss when she checked her emails, and read mine. Now she was taking my email to show him. Yes, my email! It appeared the dream was very significant after all.

It wasn't until early afternoon that she contacted me with a full explanation. Apparently, after reading my correspondence, her boss had said, 'When can you bring her over here?' I was stunned. Why would they want me in Munich?

Josie explained that she had been given a promotion and needed to select three out of six countries in her new portfolio. In my dream I had described the Dubai office to a tee, and Christmas time was significant in her long-term goals for this country. Her boss had added jokingly, 'Could she also help you select the two other countries?' After all, her success would be his success.

'Can you help me, Georgina?' I kept hearing in one ear, while in my other ear, spirit was saying, 'You must tell her the rest of the dream—tell her!'

I started typing: 'There was something I omitted from the dream, Josie. There was an ex-boyfriend named Ralph. I was lonely so I rushed to kiss him. As I moved forward he smiled and all his teeth were rotten. I jumped back.' After describing the dream, I asked her: 'Josie, by any chance is there a Ralph connected to one of these six countries? Your wanting to rush things by selecting the wrong country could have a major impact on your success.'

Within minutes my mobile was ringing. This was far too confidential to place in an email, Josie said. Then she blurted out that Ralph was the boss of the office in one of those countries. We discussed the options, and I also explained that rotten teeth were not a good omen. At the end of the conversation, Josie invited me to have a holiday with her and her family in Germany.

Her invitation was alluring. Things were stirring within my soul. I knew that once, in a past life, I had been of the Jewish faith. I had always felt a deep affinity for Judaism and the Jewish thread in my life had surfaced in all kinds of ways: As a child I'd often come out with words in Hebrew. When I was growing up there was no television or friends to influence or teach me that language or faith, so how did I know those words? It was accepted that they were memories from a lifetime ago.

Maybe a trip to Germany would allow me to put to rest some of the unsettling feelings and flashbacks that I'd experienced because of this previous life? It had become a familiar feature of my work that dreams for clients led to overseas vacations that in turn revealed memories and stirrings from my past lives. I had come to realise that perhaps this was spirit's way of healing my soul, or reintroducing me into the lives of people with whom I'd been connected previously. I'd already seen how the past helped grow my understanding of this lifetime and benefited from the lessons that would come from these understandings.

I thanked Josie for her invitation and agreed to investigate the options. I thought that perhaps I could attend a workshop while I was there. It would balance out the social side of the trip.

Several years back, I had attended a workshop, which I loved, with Rosalyn Bruyere in the US and I knew she conducted workshops in Germany every year. As if divinely conspired, she just happened to be holding a workshop at the exact time I planned to visit Josie.

The workshop was about the Mystery Schools of Egypt—spot on! Interestingly, Rosalyn's husband was of the Jewish faith.

But even more was to unfold. About five weeks prior to leaving for Germany, I had just hopped into bed and was having quiet time, reflecting on the day's events, when a golden light appeared in the corner of my bedroom. I turned and saw someone in spirit form, wearing a long robe. I couldn't see their face, as a shimmering gold light was covering it. The spirit had one arm outstretched, as if pointing to a place or direction, and I heard the words, 'Go towards Aaron'. That was all. Nothing more, nothing less.

I couldn't sleep. What was the significance of Aaron? I knew from my long-ago days at Sunday school that he was the brother of Moses—a high priest and prophet, who could turn a rod into a snake. But, when I later asked some of my friends about this, I got a surprise: I was told that the Maronite church dates back to pre-Arab Semitic times and its followers believe they are descendants of the Canaanites, thereby holding sacred the celebration of Moses and Aaron. They claim the Festival of the Cross in September for celebrating their connections to the past—the very month I was leaving for Germany.

Hmmm . . . interesting. The threads were coming together. I was going to Germany, attending a workshop with a theme of Egypt, the country from which Moses and Aaron led the exodus of the Israelites to the promised land. So there was a connection for me between Egypt, Germany and the Jewish faith.

It was so good to see Josie again, and meet her husband Heinz. I could easily see why Josie had fallen for him—he was tall, blond and very handsome! As we sat eating our first meal together, I had a sudden image of him in a Nazi uniform. I felt spirit was showing me that his family had a past link to the regime. I quickly pushed aside the vision. The conversation was centred around my beliefs, my research and how I sensed that in a past life I had been a Jew on a train heading towards a concentration camp. Fear flashed in Heinz's eyes as I spoke. I knew then that the picture I had seen was right!

Later, when I had Josie to myself, I confided to her what I had seen and enquired whether Heinz's grandfather had been a superior in Hitler's regime.

'We only found out recently ourselves, Georgina,' she admitted. 'Much was hidden by his family. His mum was going through old photos after her father died and she uncovered photos and memorabilia of those dark days. Heinz is ashamed he has such a heritage.'

Heinz looked relieved during breakfast the next morning when I spoke about healing and letting go of the past. I explained that my research was not about anger, but about understanding the energies that may still be lingering in the surroundings and buildings of that era after such horrendous acts. The pain left his face and he felt encouraged that he could be the catalyst for healing within his own family.

Germany was everything the soul could have hoped for—green, lush, clean and orderly. It was early autumn and the weather was wonderful as we holidayed around the lakes and the mountains. Oktoberfest was in full swing and through Heinz's work associations, we had a special booth in one of the pavilions in which to celebrate. It was absolutely incredible.

It was to be a slower pace as I headed off to Kisslegg for the workshop. The train trip showed me places I never expected to see. But there was a stirring as I heard the sounds of the train on the track and viewed the landscape. It was my memory of a time when I was piled into a train, compressed with numerous others, on a death ride. I wanted to forget, but the feeling was so crippling, so sad. I had to get up and stretch my legs to shift the scene and dissipate the memories from my mind.

There was a hitch at the workshop that, I must admit, I should have thought about—the majority of people attending spoke only German. Rosalyn gave her lectures in English, and her husband translated them into German, but break times were quite challenging. Fortunately, several attendees were fluent in both languages and at times offered their services as an interpreter, so I could join in on group conversations.

One of the people who was able to speak German and English was Marion, and we soon became friends, talking about old churches, architecture and the unusual. After an early breakfast each morning, we would head off into one of the adjoining villages to see what we could find. We came across a black Madonna in one church, we found a saint's skeletal remains in a glass coffin in another, and on another morning a church was filled with the melodic tones of the choir rehearsing in their own dialect. It sent goosebumps down our spines.

I left the workshop feeling charged and invigorated for the next part of my research, Dachau. Unlike my previous train trip, the journey back to Munich was very entertaining—as the train pulled into each little village station, more people would hop on, and everyone was in party mode, heading to Munich's Oktoberfest. There were young children, teenagers and adults, all so happy and full of enthusiasm and dressed in traditional-style clothes. I loved the men's hats, with an assortment of feathers off to one side. Some even wore hand-knitted long socks, but I giggled silently to myself—they might have been wearing woollen socks and leather shorts, but how did they keep their legs warm on the cold nights?

The lady sitting next to me could speak English and explained that there was also a very special event happening that weekend in some of the villages, to celebrate the bringing down of the cheeses that had been curing in the mountains. In the old days, the farmers used cheese as a form of currency, so when they sold their cheese in the villages it meant they would have money to spend to celebrate. This tradition has been carried forward in the form of a festival in many of the more traditional villages. I was learning that the Germans loved any excuse to enjoy their beer!

On the tour to Dachau, I was among a mixed lot from a variety of nations and ages. Our guide was an American who had fallen in love with a German lass and ended up staying in Munich. There was little time to rest as we were off one train and onto another, then a quick walk to the other side of the railway station to catch a local bus. Before we reached our destination, my head started to pound. I felt like I was going to explode. I knew that I was tapping into something, but what?

Then the bus stopped and our guide assembled us on the side of the road. He explained that we had just driven through the housing estate where the Nazi officers and their families lived. I realised that my psychic radar was honing in on the imbalance of energy created by the events that had taken place here. Although this wasn't the actual concentration camp, those working at the camp would have brought home the dark energies they'd accumulated there. It was very unpleasant but, after all, that's what I had come to observe, feel and sense.

As we reached the main front gate where the prisoners had entered the camp, you couldn't help but notice it carried the words *Arbeit macht frei*, meaning 'work makes you free'. It was a sombre moment. We were taken to a section of the camp that was rebuilt in 2003 to show visitors the path of the arrivals to the camp.

Dachau was the first concentration camp for political prisoners and opened in March 1933, just a few weeks after Hitler came to power. It served as a model for those built by the Nazis across Germany and Europe. The first people rounded up and sent to Dachau were political opponents of the fascist regime, including communist party members and social-democrats, trade union leaders, liberals, artists, writers and musicians, many of whom were Jews. As our guide showed us through the camp, including its crematoria, I felt overwhelmed by the sheer enormity of human loss. More than 200,000 prisoners were incarcerated there between 1933 and 1945, with an estimated 41,500 murdered.

Since the original camp had been torn down, the barracks displayed a cross-section of the camp, showing what the living conditions were like for the prisoners. I felt sick when I saw some of the tools of punishment on display and hurriedly passed by for some fresh air outside. There were no other buildings, just 32 slabs of concrete where other barracks once stood.

A number of religious groups had built memorials to those who had died. As I walked through the grounds, I felt nothing of what I had anticipated. On the bus ride through the town I had picked up the dark and disturbing energies of the officers, but in the grounds themselves the residual energy felt quite different. This place, a site of so much pain and suffering by the innocent, had a silence that left me feeling numb.

I had seen enough, but I was drawn to cross a small canal that acted like a moat with tall barbed wire fences on either side. There was a beautiful green forest to the right and I could see some seats. I welcomed the thought of some quiet contemplation. The trees were refreshing and a break from the starkness of the camp. Suddenly, I had the most intense pain go through my back—straight through, and not just in one place but in numerous areas. The pain was so severe it made me dizzy; I had to find a seat, and fast.

I couldn't understand what I had just experienced. I wondered if I had picked up a memory of someone being shot or executed in these woods. Finally, when I felt I had gained enough composure, I found my group. It was time to leave. I asked the guide whether the forest had any significance to the camp. He said it was an escape route that many prisoners had chosen to use; they knew they may not reach freedom but would rather be shot than experience a slow death in the camp.

That explained why I picked up a snapshot of the past there. I suspect the woods had not been cleansed of their residual memory as they lay outside the compounds of the concentration camp. The earth and trees still contained the memory bank of history, stored at a cellular level. It reminded me how often nature suffers at the hands of man. Although the forest looked inviting, a sensitive such as myself could tap into the experiences of the past. I had discovered what I was looking for—proof of residual energy of what had happened at Dachau.

I was exhausted by the time I arrived back at Josie and Heinz's home. It had been a day of emotionally charged activities, but they were keen to hear of my findings. Heinz, in particular, showed much enthusiasm when I told him I'd learned that every school child in Germany, as part of their education, must go on an excursion to one concentration camp, so the tragic events might never happen again in their country. This gave him great hope for the future of his own child, and his people.

Even the saddest locations and darkest places can be healed, though it may take many attempts to lift the residual energy. If you are trying to remove negative energy from an area or premises, don't stop with just one session—you may need several, depending on the depth of emotion. A few tips: have the area or premises prayed over and blessed by a holy person; sprinkle with holy water; burn sage or a smudge stick; change the frequencies in the air by clapping your hands or using a tuning fork or a Tibetan prayer ball or gong. Remember to open all doors and windows in dwellings to allow the fresh air to enter and push the toxic energies out. Most importantly, cleanse yourself before and after these sessions—you don't want to be taking home any negative energies that may have jumped on you.

25

FULL CIRCLE

It doesn't matter who you are or how far you've travelled, life will always throw you a curved ball now and then. My apartment was full of unpacked boxes and the only chair I could find had been plonked by the removalist right in front of the television set. I sat motionless. I had exhausted all my tears. The background sounds from the rambling TV felt like a moth was in my ears, fluttering, aggravating, trying to stir any spare energy I had. But I had nothing left to give.

The last fortnight had been manic with the move to a new apartment in a new suburb. I had allowed a two-week overlap to move my precious items and clothing, and to set up my reading room for my clients. Time was running out before I was off overseas, once again for the Middle East, to Israel. There wasn't much time to think about anything else.

Thankfully, I'd decided to make Mum's 86th birthday treat two weeks earlier than her actual birthday. We'd gone to Far North Queensland to visit my youngest son and his new family. Although she was getting more frail, Mum's anticipation before the trip was child-like and it turned out to be everything she had hoped for.

I remember my dear friend Louise saying before I left, 'Don't forget to take plenty of photos.' And that I did. There were the videos of Mum singing to her granddaughter Claira, restaurant photos with the family and more. It was a trip of a lifetime for her and she didn't stop talking about it when we got home!

I now see that over those previous weeks spirit had been preparing Mum for another journey—that of the psychic traveller. She lived by herself and would still drive to the local shop. When she told me that her disability sticker kept falling off the windscreen, I urged her to go to the local motor registry to get a new cover for the sticker. A few weeks later I asked her if she had followed through with my suggestion and she responded with a firm, precise, 'No, I've been told I won't need it'. This surprised me, but I knew she meant that spirit had told her she would no longer need her sticker, and with all the busyness in my life, I didn't give it too much thought. Later, I realised this was my first sign from spirit.

Mum had wanted her own spending money for the trip to Queensland and asked me to take her to the bank so she could withdraw some spare cash. I was stunned at the amount she took out, as the holiday was a gift and she didn't need any money. But again, she was firm. Hardly any money was spent and a large sum returned home with her. At least she would have ample cash for weeks of housekeeping and bills, I thought.

With the daily quick trips to the new apartment while I was moving, I'd frequently drop in and have a chat and coffee with Mum. One particular day, she asked if I was okay for money. She wanted to show me where she had hidden the leftover cash from our holiday. It certainly was an unusual hiding place, sandwiched between the old faded ballerina table placemats of my youth, resting on top of her china cabinet. In hindsight, this was sign number two.

Sign three was rather pointed and it did take me by surprise at the time. Mum wasn't the most demonstrative type of person, probably due to her English background. I quite clearly remember her saying to me that week, 'I know you love me'. Although it warmed my heart, something rang an alarm within my soul that this was unusual. My mother preferred actions over words.

I was physically drained and my back was giving way so I missed the usual drop-in. I had seen Mum on the Monday and she was in a hurry, off to visit her doctor. We had time for a quick chat and coffee. I watched her leave for the doctor's, wearing a plastic rain hat and her green overcoat, and packing up her walking stick and trolley bag into her little white car. Off she drove, leaving me to lock up her house. That would be the last time I saw her alive.

Several days passed and I returned to hand over the keys of the old apartment and finally leave the suburb I'd grown up in. It was time for a new direction. I felt that, with the move, a chapter had closed in my life. Without realising it, I had tapped into a prediction that was about to unfold—but my life was about to change a whole lot more.

I called in to speak to Mum, expecting the usual warm greeting on her face to welcome me. It was a tradition that she accompanied me as I drove down her driveway. Mum had an eagle eye out for activities in the street and very good hearing, so she always knew I'd arrived. But there was no sign of her. I knocked on the front door. There was no answer. The garage door was closed, which meant she was inside.

I never took her house keys with me when I visited because she was always there. Fortunately, there was a spare set hidden near the garage. I rushed to the hiding place, only to find she had moved them. It had become a bit of a pattern in the last several years—Mum moving things and not putting them back or forgetting where she had placed them, something I had gotten accustomed to! But these keys were never supposed to be moved. For the past six years, Mum had worn an emergency alarm around her neck and one press would notify the alarm centre that she was in trouble. If she didn't pick up the phone they would call for backup, knowing where to find the keys for entry into her home.

I peered through the window of the lounge. There she was, laying on the floor in her pyjamas. I knew she had passed. She died in exactly the same spot as my father had some fifteen years earlier. It had always been her wish to die in the home they had built and lived in together for nearly 50 years. Her doctor later said she had gone within seconds, so quickly that she would not have been able to activate her emergency beeper. She died three days after her 86th birthday.

As I sat in my new apartment, there was no joy in the experience of a new beginning, as now I was faced with the loss of my mother. My loss shook me to my core, and made me question what I did and stood for, both professionally and personally. After all, I was supposed to be a gifted seer, an international psychic intuitive whose clients seek out my abilities to foresee and predict their futures—but I had not predicted this. Why had this been kept from me?

My gift as a channel and a medium forms a bridge from this world to the next—I act as the instrument or receiver to relay messages from beyond to those on earth, to confirm that the spirit world does exist and life is eternal. Sometimes answers are sought: will my beloved still be part of my life? Can they see the family and be part of our special days? Will we meet again? I spend my life giving those who are grieving messages of hope and reassurance. So where did this leave me?

I have always said busyness is deafness to the spirit world. My rushing about moving house meant that my own psychic senses hadn't been allowed to tap into what was occurring around me. Had Mum sensed her final journey was close, or was it spirit's way of making the path ready for her spiritual rebirth? Maybe this was part of the divine plan, as our journeys on earth are predetermined in the spirit world. Perhaps I wasn't meant to have a physical knowing that my mum was about to leave, to allow her an easier transition from her earthly life to the next phase of her soul's existence.

There was a fourth sign—one that later provided me with much relief. It had come from my father. I was having a remedial massage that week and the therapist, Alison, said something very profound—and she's not one for giving psychic messages offhand! 'Your father is here,' Alison told me. 'He is acknowledging the work and care you have given to your mother and that it is about to be lifted.'

It was a most perplexing message at the time, but within 24 hours Mum passed away. Dad's spirit was preparing me for what he could see and knew would be her final journey on earth. How comforting now to know that all is planned minutely. Mum's exit point was already chosen and I sense that she, too, knew this.

Could I have done anything to prevent this from occurring? This is a natural question, one that many, many clients ask me when they have a Dearly Departed session. The answer, as I have discovered myself, is usually no; there's nothing any of us can do. When your final exit point has arrived your soul is ready for its journey home to find peace, healing and reconnection to loved ones past.

I was lucky that the subject of death was openly talked about when I was growing up. I was raised with a firm Christian Spiritualist background. Our beliefs were strong and we knew that when the physical body dies, the soul is in a continuum, existing in another dimension. In some ways, it's like living in another room of your house. You're still connected, although you may feel separated. Mum used to say her physical body was a casing and once it was shed, her soul was free to soar to another dimension, heaven.

In my professional life as a psychic medium I have daily proof of the ongoing existence of loved ones in spirit; I communicate with those who have departed, who in turn relay their messages to their beloved sitting in front of me. Now, I too was faced with the question—who would give me that same form of warmth, bond and confirmation of eternal life?

Then it happened! There was the most vivid blue, electric light, flashing, yet so small. It was about the size of an adult thumb, surrounded by the whitest of white iridescent lights. It was strobing, flashing, buzzing. I was reminded of the fairies that fly around in children's movies. Mum was trying to get my attention. This was truly a spirit form. The light buzzed towards my forehead and I felt immense peace, love, comfort and warmth. I knew my mother's soul, or spirit, had heard my prayers and through my inner thoughts she had now come to comfort and nurture me once more.

I had been remorseful that day. I was overcome with guilt about not picking up that she had died. Why hadn't I sensed something? I was feeling overwhelmed and a failure in my chosen profession. I imagine it's much like a doctor would feel if, with all their training, skill and enlightenment, they didn't diagnose or couldn't save a loved one.

Backtracking, I was able to pinpoint her time of death to within 30 minutes. Mum loved a particular television show at 5.30 p.m. She would sit down with her evening meal and watch the program and at 6 p.m. exactly—she was programmed for detail—she would take a pill. When I found her she had partly eaten her soup, her chips were still in the microwave and she hadn't taken her pill. Thanks to her predictability, these details gave me the answer I needed regarding the time of her passing.

FULL CIRCLE

I remember that evening clearly. I watched a different show at that time, and when visiting each other Mum and I often would often debate about who was going to watch their show. On reflection, on the night of her passing, as I was watching the program, I suddenly got the most violent headache. I remember grabbing my head and even taking painkillers.

Obviously, this moment was Mum's physical point of separation from the earth plane. In her wisdom, she would have known that after finding her I would be full of stress, grief and dislocation. She would have preferred me to have a good night's sleep in preparation for what was to come. So true—I didn't sleep for two days afterwards.

When I was growing up, Mum always said that she was my teacher and although my gifts took me in different directions as I matured—I embraced all religions and she stayed true to her Christian beliefs—the common denominator was that we both believed that we all come from spirit/heaven and would return to spirit/heaven. Now, for the first time in my life, my mother would not be around to discuss psychic phenomena with me. Would her role as my instructor continue from the other side? These are the kinds of questions we all struggle with when we lose someone close.

My answer was to come through one of my dearest friends, Louise, a brilliant psychic medium. It is best if I let Louise tell you in her words the story of how spirit had perfectly timed a message for both of us. This is what she wrote about the passing of my mum, Agnes.

'Six months before Agnes—my dear mentor and friend, who was also a medium and great healer—passed away, I was asked if I wished to undertake a reading with a UK medium when they arrived in

Australia. I never really seek the services of another medium (given I am one myself), even though I have lost a brother, a sister figure and a close aunt and grandmother. Yet I felt that I should accept the offer and I entered a date and time into my diary.

'On the week of Agnes passing away, I noticed that the timeslot I had written down in my diary many months before was a couple of hours before her funeral. I was asked to do a speech for Agnes at the service and I knew in my heart that the spirit world had preordained the psychic reading beforehand for a reason. I decided to quickly attend the reading before I went to the funeral. I would have just enough time to drive back for the service.

'The UK medium knew nothing about me. We had never met. Immediately Agnes made herself known and the bond between us three mediums became apparent. The excitement flowed through my veins as I reconnected with Agnes via someone else. The medium was able to describe Agnes's looks, how she dressed, and that she was a poetess. Agnes conveyed that she was surprised to see how much she was loved. I now knew what needed to be said about Agnes at her service and, true to her personality, she would have liked to have the last word!

'Agnes was English and followed the traditional spiritualist movement's teachings which originated there. Ironically, the medium who conducted my reading was also English. The last time I had seen Agnes alive on this side was some weeks before when she watched me demonstrate to a large audience with another well-known UK medium. I knew this was a wonderful gift from the spirit world for the many decades she had served as a clear channel for countless hurting souls. I left the stage at intermission and the only people I visited and kissed in the audience were Agnes and Georgina. It was to be our final farewell. The story of Agnes's passing is a prime example that we are all connected and so much of our life is preordained, including our departure.'

So yet again Mum had reached out from the afterlife. I felt comforted. She was still my teacher and now my spiritual guide.

26

THE PILGRIMAGE

I was to leave for Israel in less than two weeks. It would be the Jewish Passover and the Christian Easter, two very significant events for my research on spirituality. I contemplated cancelling but then it dawned on me—this had been Mum's wish. Mum had always hoped I would walk the path of her king, Jesus. Her words came flooding back to me and I felt I needed to say goodbye to her in a way that she would have loved. So my psychic travelling journey was also to become a pilgrimage to take some of my mother's ashes to her master's resting place and for me to say a final farewell.

The funeral was Thursday and I was to leave the following Tuesday. The crematorium arranged for me to collect the ashes late on Monday. My son had shown me how to take the seal off the ashes box, enabling me to fill a small porcelain rosary container, adorned with a beautiful dove of peace on the lid, which I had bought especially for the trip. Opening the seal seemed as though it would be easy, but once I was by myself I didn't have the strength or energy to remove it. Here I was, in the kitchen of my new apartment, surrounded with unpacked boxes and no device to manipulate the seal. The screwdriver that my son had used when showing me what to do was at Mum's house, not my apartment. I tried a knife, but that bent. As I held the large box of ashes, engraved with the name Agnes Gibson, tears flooded down my face and I cried out to my mother: 'If you want to go with me to Israel, help me get some of you into this pot.'

Suddenly I heard the word 'scissors'. I did have a large pair of scissors at the apartment to cut open the boxes I'd used for moving. Magically, or perhaps divinely inspired, I was able to cut the seal, the top flipped off easily and I transferred some of Mum's ashes into the rosary container. It was small enough to fit in my handbag and I hoped that customs officers wouldn't think that I was transporting an illegal substance! I prayed that Mum would make sure there were no such occurrences on this journey, and there weren't.

Peering through the windows of the plane as we started our descent, I noticed rays of sun spilling through the clouds in the sky. I likened it to energy, fingers of gold on a land that held much mystery. I started to feel it was right for me to be there.

I had planned two weeks in Israel, but the reality of losing someone so dear made this trip harder than the others. With knee replacement surgery scheduled in six months, I needed a walking stick to get around; plus I was feeling the effects of the exhaustion of the preceding weeks, the move and the passing of Mum. Now also jet-lagged, I cried myself to sleep on a number of nights.

Anyone who has been on a guided day tour knows they go at a feverish pace. The trips were far too fast. Hiring a car was out of the question—it seemed as if road rules didn't exist, or were made up on the spot! So each day I would take Mum's ashes in my bag, hoping there'd be a particular spot that had religious significance where I could scatter them.

With only one more tour left, one more opportunity to scatter the ashes, I prayed to Mum for an opportunity on the next day's excursion where I could scatter her ashes over the water. The last trip was up the coast towards Lebanon, with nothing out of the Bible that she would have felt connected to. I would have loved Galilee or Jerusalem, but that was not to be. However, I was to learn that spirit had a way when there seemed no way!

The excursion was once again so fast that some people asked the guide to slow down because of my disability, but she had a schedule to keep! My ears pricked up when I heard her inform us that we would be driving through a place by the sea mentioned in the Bible. I felt relieved. 'Thank you, thank you,' I said to Mum. It had some religious connection, even if only a tiny one.

I started to unwrap the mounds of tape from around the porcelain container but when I noticed that it had broken in two, I panicked. I would need plenty of time to carefully unwrap the tape to avoid losing any of the container's precious contents prior to scattering. Time to enjoy the sights was always cut short and rushed, there were never enough minutes in the tour to enjoy the attractions you had signed on for—so how on earth would I have time for this delicate task?

My father had requested that his ashes be scattered at sea. We often joked between ourselves that it would be my luck that the wind would blow them right back onto me. However, it had been Mum's wish to scatter his ashes in silence and by herself. It wasn't the silence she had hoped for, though. Dad and Mum walked at a particular ocean park daily. After his passing, she decided to scatter his ashes there one morning. She, too, had trouble lifting the lid off the box and had to return to the car to use a screwdriver to remove it. Putting the large box in a carry bag, she started walking through the park when a familiar walking buddy enquired where my dad was. Mum didn't want to say he was in a box in the bag now hanging from her arm, which his dogs were circling and sniffing! Brushing off this acquaintance, she moved closer to the water's edge and scattered Dad's ashes as far as she could. Unfortunately, not all of them went into the sea—some lay on the rocks. Tossing and turning during the night, she was very concerned that the ashes may not be taken out to sea in the high tide. On returning the next morning to inspect the area, she was relieved to see the waves had taken the ashes away. Now, in Israel, history was about to repeat itself.

It was a magical, beautiful scene, as if Mum had hand-picked the place herself. And there was an additional blessing of free time to explore on our own! But the steps to the water were wet and slimy from the high tide of the Mediterranean Sea. It was a tricky balancing act: walking stick, handbag and partly unwrapped broken porcelain container of ashes.

I found the perfect site—a grotto where the water was so blue, serene and transparent—and said a silent prayer. Then, to my utter dismay, I saw that the ashes had partly moved from the container onto the plastic cling-wrap. I could hear a group of tourists coming closer. I had to act, as I only had seconds to do what I longed for. So in it all went into the water—the container, the ashes and the plastic. I am usually very environmentally conscious, but at this point my emotional needs were overriding sensibility!

They were gone—but not completely. There, in front of me, were some of Mum's ashes laying on the rocks that formed a barrier between the viewing platform and the sea. I quickly tried to brush them into the water before the tourist group arrived. Their tour leader asked if I'd like my photo taken. The photo says it all—I look guilty! Then my own tour guide turned up, and seeing that I looked rather stressed, enquired what the matter was. Either she didn't understand my Australian accent or she was in disbelief. Her face remained motionless and she walked away, perhaps leaving me to be in the moment.

Finally Mum was home in the land she felt deeply connected to. Had she scripted this trip to time with her own departure? She had written a poem for her 85th birthday and recited it to her church family:

I'm 85 terday, yoo-hoo, yes I'm 85 terday
So now you can give me the key to this door
Cos I've never been 85 before
But I'm a clever old girl and I know a few tricks
So I've put me name down for 86.

THE PILGRIMAGE

I can see there's a cake with bright coloured candles
The food looks delicious but you all look so hungry
Please leave some for me cos I need it for strength
To put on me joggers to run till I'm spent.

I do blame me joggers cos they just won't stop
They just keep on humming clipperty clop
And then they smarten up and get me into gear.

Anyway thanks for the party which is to come
Now I must hasten away to listen for the starter's gun
And when I hear it there will be no stopping me
I'll be off and away on my great super run.

Mum was blessed with another year and three days—enough time for me to unknowingly take part in her script and exit point. She had become part of my play; my script as the psychic traveller.

27

THE SECRET OF BETHLEHEM

Tel Aviv, a city that doesn't sleep, was a great place to base myself for tours. I stayed at an amazing boutique hotel that was once a cinema. It still held the charm and character of the original building, with detailed photographs and old cinema equipment scattered throughout the hotel and a museum in honour of its heritage.

I was told that a visit to the old part of the city was a must—to see the beautiful architecture, the history and the shopping. It felt like an Eastern bazaar—old-wares dealers, rug stalls, jewellery makers and antique bric-a-brac scattered among gelato bars and Arabic nut sellers. Diversification of faiths was in harmony—Jewish, Muslim and Christian working side by side.

I even found a fortune-teller, near the old clock tower building. He reminded me of Einstein with his salt and pepper fuzzy hair as he peered down over his glasses as if to read your soul. Patience was needed as he already had a client with him, so I busied myself talking to the chap who was waiting for his friend. He told me what to expect—a mixture of palmistry, numerology and astrology—and the fee the fortune-teller charged.

When it was my turn I walked up the tiny staircase that weaved around several storeys to meet . . . let's call him the nutty professor. He had a string of qualifications on his business card but what struck me was the incorrect spelling, which was surprising as he was supposed to be so well educated!

He certainly hit the mark on several aspects, but kept asking questions, which a psychic should never do unless, for example, a birth date is needed to work out the numerology or astrological energies. Then he quoted a fee for removing the curse or curses he saw in my life—I stopped him right there.

My lesson that day was not about my future but how someone can be so manipulative in conning decent folk out of their hard-earned dollars. He preyed on the vulnerable, the weak, the broken-hearted. There was no light or goodness in what he did. I was relieved to leave.

I continued my way through the markets and came to a man repairing carpets—it was really a privilege to sit down and watch as he patiently weaved his magic in and out of the missing looms of wool or silk. This was a man of integrity who could see the beauty in what was once a magnificent work of art and wished to restore it to a fine showpiece—not like the fortune-teller who had sold his soul.

My trip to Israel included an invitation to attend a friend's son's bar mitzvah, the Jewish ritual that celebrates a boy's passage into manhood. The taxi dropped me off on the outskirts of Tel Aviv at a small synagogue. Everyone was welcoming and warm. Although the service was not in English, the energies of the words, the emotions of the songs and the ritual made me cry. I cried tears of joy for hearing the words I had once spoken lifetimes ago, I cried for the beauty of the service, I cried for the freshness of youth—the hopes they held for tomorrow. In our busy lives we seemed to have lost touch with rituals and traditions, but regardless of culture or faith, rites of passage remain a significant benchmark in the stages of ageing. We have lost the ability to celebrate the milestones of life, celebrate family and celebrate faith. I felt blessed to be part of the richness of that day.

Jerusalem was a highlight of my stay—the Mount of Olives, the Dome of the Rock, the Garden of Gethsemane and walls of the Old City. At the Wailing Wall I made my way to the women's section and placed my hand on the wall, giving a silent thanks for the safety of my trip and saying prayers for the future.

Then it was on to the Christian quarter to follow the route of the Via Dolorosa, tracing Jesus' steps to the site of his crucifixion at the Church of the Holy Sepulchre. It was here at the church that I had an experience I had not anticipated.

I had placed myself in a very quiet part of the church, away from the packed crowds, to have some quiet time and see if I was able to tap into any remaining memories or feelings of the past. Suddenly, I became outraged. I looked at the people passing me and, to be frank, I wanted to punch and scream at them. I literally hated them! This was totally out of character for me. Then I realised that the experience and emotions were not mine, nor did they belong to the people walking past me—they were the energies of the people of the time when Christ was crucified, or afterwards when the Christian Crusaders made their mark. I was not in a happy place when the bus pulled up at the border between Israel and Palestine.

We hurried off the bus to the checkpoint; the entry point into Palestine. Border patrol officers with large guns surveyed our every move. We were told to hurry and not to loiter as we made our way down the corridor of barbed wire to the waiting hire cars. It was a scary experience.

The desert was mountainous—peaks and troughs, arid and dusty. Our cars stopped outside the courtyard of Manger Square that led to the Church of the Nativity. The structure is built over a cave that tradition marks as the birthplace of Jesus of Nazareth, sacred to Christians. The heavy wooden door leading into the church is only 120 centimetres high, and somewhat of a squeeze for me. I loved the beautiful mosaics along the walls and floor on the way to altar. There were two sets of stairs, one on either side of the altar, that led down into the Grotto of the Nativity, where Jesus was born. A silver star embedded in white marble marked the exact spot—it felt magical and still. Many people dropped down to their knees and kissed the star in reverence.

Before leaving we were given free time to explore the numerous chapels or take in the breathtaking view of the valley where, it is said, the three wise men saw the star in the sky that led them to the birthplace of Jesus. There was something so significant there—an energy, a vortex, which I had only ever felt once before, and that was in Great Zimbabwe. It was the Circle of Life, where the beginning meets the end.

Had the divine powers of the spirit world chosen Bethlehem to be the birthplace for change due to the incredible vortex power that existed there?

Whatever your belief system may be, you could feel the power of this place. No wonder religious wars are fought over this humble land. There is great significance and potential in the energy, the vortex that draws people to Bethlehem. It has powers—supernatural powers—that combine together to make history now and in the future.

I left feeling at peace. I had uncovered something of a secret, a natural phenomenon beyond religion that perhaps ancient man once understood.

Thankfully, I had allocated some rest days in Tel Aviv before heading home, as I had much to absorb about my new trains of thought. On my last day I was off to Caesarea, the beautiful fishing port that was transformed into a Roman capital by King Herod. The ancient archaeological ruins made me feel like I was still visiting a Roman city, majestically sitting on the edge of the Mediterranean Sea, where people came to socialise and bathe in the mosaic-tiled pools and baths... those days were grand, opulent, decadent.

It was in the former Crusader city of Acre that I felt the past—chilling, cold and noisy. Today, the city is a bewildering network of narrow streets, largely an eighteenth-century Turkish town built on the ruins of the old city. But below is another world—the Underground City—fashioned well below street level. It was the home of the Crusaders, who made Acre their main stronghold and link between the Latin kingdom and Europe. They referred to it as St Jean d'Acre.

There was cool relief from the heat of the day as we descended the tiny stairs to observe the Crusader architecture that once housed the Hospitallers of St John of Jerusalem, a chivalrous order concerned with the health and spiritual welfare of pilgrims. I could hear footsteps and noises, not of the people in the tour group, but similar to those made by the Viking spirits of Dublin. Again, the energies of the former occupiers of this city were strong. These ancient guardians of the faith were still very much spiritually in charge of their city. I couldn't understand the language or speech, but the energy was one of excitement; animated and at times argumentative. I got flashes of what some of the Crusaders looked like as well. They were smaller in stature than I had anticipated, and I was also taken aback by the number of them who had red hair!

My concentration was broken when the guide beckoned me to join the group once more. The underground city is still alive with energies of the past, so if you have a chance to, spend some time in the underground chambers, touch the architecture and you may have a spiritual encounter like no other! I felt privileged that I had been given a window into the past.

As I continued on to Mount Carmel and other landmarks I realised my trip had become a pilgrimage of faith. Not just one faith but the faith of the people who had walked these tribal lands for centuries: the Arabs, Jews and later Christians. It was a spiritual encounter. My emotions had been like a pendulum, swinging from anger and resentment at Jerusalem, to a sense of reverence at Bethlehem. I'd experienced polar opposites. And I came to realise that Israel was a reflection of the world. Nothing has really changed.

As psychic travellers we seek the cosmic truth about why we are here and what we have to learn to progress in this life and the next. The world is still turning and wars are still being fought—when will we learn the lessons of the past? Wherever you are, use every opportunity you have in your everyday life to keep asking the important questions; and never forget that the answer lies within you.

RESOURCES

Books

Evans, Annie, *Live The Life You Long For*, Allen & Unwin, Sydney, Australia, 2010, pages 27, 28

Matthews, Caitlin, *The Psychic Protection Handbook*, Piatkus Books Ltd, London, UK, 2005

Nabokov, Isabelle, *Religion Against the Self: An Ethnography of Tamil Rituals*, Oxford University Press, New York, 2000

Newton, Michael, *Journey of Souls*, Llewellyn Publications, Woodbury, MN, USA, 2009

Walker, Georgina, *Dearly Departed: Everything You Want to Know About the Afterlife,* Allen & Unwin, Sydney, Australia, 2006

Winkowski, Mary Ann, *When Ghosts Speak*, Hachette Australia, Sydney, Australia, 2007

Magazines

Walker, Georgina, 'Vikings in Dublin', *New Idea*, Pacific Magazines, Sydney [2004]
Skyhost Magazine, Gecko Publishing, August–September 2010

Websites

Celtic Spirit Band, 'Customs of Ireland', www.celticspiritband.com/customs.htm [11 January 2012]
Colm Moriarty, 'Dublin's Viking Warrior Burials', bit.ly/zrURYr [10 January 2012]
Crocodile victim survived Bali blast, www.shm.com.au/articles/2002/10/26/1035504922426 [22 April 2012]
Dave Juliano, 'The Shadowlands', theshadowlands.net/ghost/residual.htm [10 January 2012]
Game Reserve, 'Zimbabwe: Hwange National Park', game-reserve-com/zimbabwe-Hwange_np.html [19 February 2012]
Journeys, 'Workshop', www.journeysmyanmar.com/nat_workshop.htm [13 February 2012]
Murong Gallery, 'Reviews on Stone', www.murongogallery.com/catalog/content.php?id=varied_reviews_on_stone_s [15 February 2012]
New Zealand Herald, 'Avalanche Victim Escaped Death Only Three Weeks Ago', www.nzherald.co.nz/nz/news/article.cfm?c_id=1&objectid=10591165 [16 August 2009]
Out-Of-Body Experiences and Lucid Dreams, www.lucidity.com/NL.32.OBEandLD.html [20 April 2012]
Parthena Black, 'Can Dreams Predict the Future?', Mind Power News, www.mindpowernews.com/DreamPredictFuture.htm [8 January 2012]
Sowmya, 'Thought is a Living Force', flavoursofindia.tripod.com/thoughts.html [8 March 2010]
The Hide Safari Park, 'The Hide', www.thehide.com/hwange.html [19 February 2012]
Viator Inc., 'Viator Tours', www.viator.com [5 March 2012]
Wikipedia, 'Astral Projection', en.wikipedia.org/wiki/Astral_projection [3 February 2012]
Wikipedia, 'Bar Mitzvah', en.wikipedia/org/wiki/Bar_Bat_Mitzvah [4 March 2012]
Wikipedia, 'Church of the Nativity', en.wikipedia.org/wiki/Church_of_the_Nativity [25 February 2012]
Wikipedia, 'Dachau Concentration Camp', en.wikipedia.org/wiki/Dachau_concentration_camp [25 February 2012]
Wikipedia, 'Great Zimbabwe', en.wikipedia.org/wiki?Great_Zimbabwe [17 February 2012]
Wikipedia, 'History of Jerusalem', en.wikipedia.org/wiki/History_of_Jerusalem [25 February 2012]

RESOURCES

Wikipedia, 'Magic (Paranormal)', en.wikipedia.org/wiki/Magic_(paranormal) [21 February 2012]
Wikipedia, 'Paranormal', en.wikipedia.org/wiki/Paranormal [14 March 2012]
Wikipedia, 'Supernatural', en.wikipedia.org/wiki/Supernatural [8 January 2010, 14 March 2012]
Wikipedia, 'Tablets of Stone', en.wikipedia.org/wiki/Tablets_of_Stone [8 March 2012]
Wikipedia, 'The Golden Rule', en.wikipedia.org/wiki?The_Golden_Rule [14 March 2012]
Wildlife, 'Animal Behaviour', animalcorner.co.uk/wildlife/elephants/elephant_famstrucbehave.html [19 February 2012]

DVD

Inca Productions, *Ghost Hunters*, Delta Entertainment, Orpington, Kent, UK, 2002

Georgina travels the world as a guest lecturer, teacher, researcher, reader, and host of Sacred Journeys. To learn more about her work and schedule please visit Georgina's website:

www.georginawalker.com

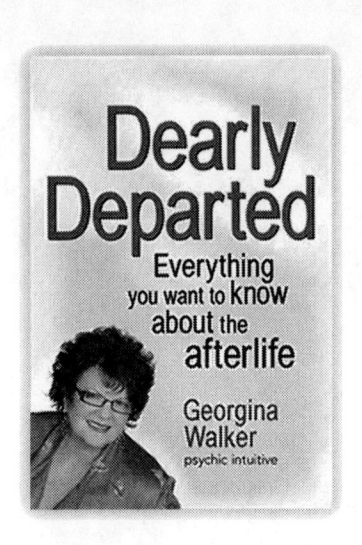

DEARLY DEPARTED
Everything you want to know about the afterlife

Where do our loved ones go when they die? What happens to our pets when they pass over? Does the soul pull away from the body before it's clinically dead? When children die, what happens to them? And what about those who suicide or are murdered? If someone you love is dying, how can you best help them? When someone we love dies there are always lots of questions. Drawing on a lifetime's experience with those who have passed over, psychic intuitive Georgina Walker shares a wealth of real life stories about the afterlife. Dearly Departed is a warm and reassuring book that deals gently and insightfully with many of the dilemmas people face around death.

AMAZING ENCOUNTERS WITH THOSE WHO HAVE PASSED OVER
And what they teach us about life after death

This heart-warming book from Georgina Walker is packed full of real-life encounters with loved ones who have passed over. Here everyday people share their remarkable stories of amazing synchronicities and unexpected moments of magic in amongst the overwhelming grief that surrounds times of separation and loss. Many accounts tell of guidance by departed loved ones, some of funny incidents that bring laughter amidst the tears. Most importantly each story contains further insights into the spirit world, showing how those who have passed on continue to take an interest in our lives.